As Far As the Eye Can See

As Far As the Eye Can See

Reflections of an Appalachian Trail Hiker
Fourth Edition

DAVID BRILL

University of Tennessee Press / Knoxville

Appalachian Trail Conservancy

Paper: 1st printing, 2013; 2nd printing, 2016.

New material is courtesy of *National Geographic Traveler* and *Smokies Life*, a publication of the Great Smoky Mountains Association, © David Brill.

TO DAD
Who taught me that compassion is at the heart
of all worthwhile journeys

I went to the woods because I wished to live deliberately, to front only the essential facts of life, and see if I could not learn what it had to teach, and not, when I came to die, discover that I had not lived.

Henry David Thoreau, *Walden*

Contents

Preface to the Fourth Edition ix

Preface to Previous Editions xiii

Acknowledgments xix

Chapter 1. Fear 1

Chapter 2. Learning to Walk, Learning to See 14

Chapter 3. Seasons 22

Chapter 4. Our Gang 32

Chapter 5. Linear Community 52

Chapter 6. Bad Company 65

Chapter 7. Sheep and Wolves 78

Chapter 8. Gear 90

Chapter 9. Stopping Along the Way 99

Chapter 10. Hot Springs Rhapsody 113

Chapter 11. Critters 123

Chapter 12. Where I Live 135

Chapter 13. Special Attractions 141

Chapter 14. Coming Home 158

Chapter 15. Appalachian Reunion: Twenty Years Later 165

Chapter 16. A Passage, at Midlife, along the Smokies AT 173

Chapter 17. On the Trail of Benton MacKaye—Again 190

Reading List 209

Preface to the Fourth Edition

 PUBLISHED *AS FAR AS THE EYE CAN SEE* **IN 1990 WITH** modest expectations, and I valued the book chiefly because it contained an enduring record of the remarkable people and events that were central to my journey on the Appalachian Trail in 1979. I never imagined the book would sell through a single printing, much less survive over 23 years and four editions. You hold in your hands a copy from the book's seventh printing. I am beyond grateful for the book's success and longevity, which, I suspect, say more about the enduring fascination with the AT than they do about my skills as a writer.

Though the book's original text has changed little, this edition contains two new chapters, in addition to the chapter on a twentieth anniversary reunion hike in Maine in 1999, which also appears in the previous edition. "A Passage at Midlife along the Smokies AT" is based on a 2008 hike of the 72 miles of the AT through Great Smoky Mountains National Park. "On the Trail of Benton MacKaye (Again)" chronicles my 2012 journey along the Benton MacKaye Trail through the Smokies, in the company of my old AT buddy Dan Howe, who is prominently featured throughout the original text. Both chapters appear at the end of this edition.

It's now been 34 years since I set out on foot, to walk from Georgia to Maine, and even after all this time, my AT experiences continue to influence my values and shape my decisions. I suspect the same is true of most, if not all, of the thousands of men and women who have followed those white blazes across 14 states.

I recently happened upon my AT journals in a trunk in the storage shed and spent an emotional few hours reading through the faded, dog-eared pages. Two entries in particular caught my attention. In the first, I express my desire to live in a cabin in the woods. The second captures my hopes to make my living as a writer.

As it turned out, both came to pass. I now live in a cabin on the Cumberland Plateau, and I've been a working journalist for more than three decades. Over the years, I've fielded hundreds of assignments, but the ones I value most have led me out into the wilds, where I've always felt most at home. Each foray into nature contributed to a rewarding life, but none will ever rival my AT experience in terms of the physical, emotional, and spiritual awakening it prompted.

It's worth noting that the central characters who grace the pages of As Far as the Eye Can See—Dan Howe, Nick Gelesko, and Paul Dillon—continue to play a vital role in my life, thanks, in part, to the modern marvel of email. Paul Dillon is now a songwriter living in Santa Fe, New Mexico. Nick, now in his 90s, and his wife, Gwen, live on the Gulf Coast of Florida. Dan Howe is the assistant city manager of Raleigh, North Carolina, with his eyes on his retirement date. In 2009, we all gathered at my cabin to celebrate the thirtieth anniversary of our hike.

Dan Howe has been a frequent guest at my home in the woods. We're now late-middle-aged dads, but whenever we bask in the light of a campfire, the AT memories tumble forth with a clarity that defies the passing years.

During my trek of the AT through Great Smoky Mountains National Park in 2008, I was in the company of that year's class of aspiring thru-hikers. My time with them demonstrated clearly that much about the AT experience has changed over the past 30-some years. Clothing and equipment have evolved from cotton and wool garments, external-frame Keltys, and cumbersome lug-soled book to Gore-Tex and fleece, sleek internal-frame packs, and footwear that more closely resembles running shoes than hiking boots. In 1979, payphones and post offices in trail towns provided our only means for communicating with friends and family back home. Today, cellular phones and other communications devices allow hikers to stay connected at their leisure, from points along the trail route.

In 1979, the majority of the trail coursed through private lands and was thus vulnerable to frequent "relos"—hiker parlance for the relocations of the trail route. Today, the AT corridor is publicly owned and protected and managed as part of the National Park System.

Despite these changes, I believe that the fundamental AT experience remains the same. Indeed, then as now, all who choose to depart a human-centric word of blacktop and steel are richly rewarded by a months-long immersion in a realm defined by daylight and darkness, the cycling of the seasons, and the dominion of nature. None arrive at the end of the journey unchanged, and for most, the changes are as profound as they are enduring.

Though each thru-hiker's experience on the trail is unique, nearly all of the published first-person accounts—which collectively have burgeoned into a literary genre—touch on a few common themes: The physical and emotional challenge of persevering through a 2,000-plus-mile journey on foot. The central role of companionship along a trail that sustains a thriving linear backwoods society. An awakening to the natural world and an evolving awareness of its myriad creatures and countless wonders. A new and perhaps more objective and better-informed perspective on the issues and problems that beset the so-called civilized world. A tendency to renounce—or at least severely challenge—a society largely predicated on status and the accumulation of material wealth. The realization that the life one left behind is less defining than the one that stretches ahead. And a tendency to scrutinize closely long-held values and beliefs and a willingness to adopt new ones that rise from what is perhaps the AT's greatest gift—the time and space to reflect, self-examine, and ultimately arrive at an enduring set of core principles.

Those precepts entered my consciousness during my 1979 hike and they remain there, still. They remain, too, on the pages of this book and the story it tells about a group of young seekers who found, if not what they were looking for, exactly what they needed—and much else besides.

David Brill
2013

Preface to Previous Editions

O N SEPTEMBER 27, 1979, I ASCENDED THE MILE-HIGH SUM-
mit of Mount Katahdin, a broad-shouldered peak
rising from the Lake Country of central Maine.
The fall frost had tinged the sugar maples bright
red, the birches shone like burnished gold, and
their color stretched away endlessly from the base of the mountain
to the horizon.

Mount Katahdin ranks as one of the more majestic peaks east
of the Mississippi, but for me it held special significance. It marked
the northern terminus of the 2,100-mile Appalachian Trail, and it
signaled the completion of a five-month journey that traced some
five million steps through the eastern wilderness over hundreds of
other peaks, through fourteen states and dozens of small mountain
towns.

When I began planning for my trek, friends and relatives seems
puzzled by my interest in forsaking the conveniences of modern
society for a months-long sojourn in the wilderness. "Why are you
doing this?" they asked, finding my commitment to the trail a bit
extreme. All I could tell them was that hiking the Appalachian
Trail was something I wanted and needed to do.

Today, I realize that my decision to hike the Appalachian Trail
wasn't as capricious as it might have seemed at the time. My pilgrimage toward the trail began years earlier, in fact, with my first
exposure to the natural world as a child and at the hand of my
grandmother.

Our family made weekly trips to her house, which sat on a quiet
street two blocks from a large, forested hill.

Each Sunday, after we had finished our early afternoon dinner, Grandma asked my brother and me if we wanted "to go up on the hill." Then, clad in her floral print dress and walking shoes, she ushered our small hiking party out the front door and toward the woods.

Through the eyes of a child, the hill loomed as large as the Appalachian peaks I would ascend years later. Though it was nothing more than a glorified nob, one of many punctuating the hilly geography of southwestern Ohio, for me it was a magical place that exposed me to countless discoveries.

Each week, as we walked along the well-worn trail, wending higher and higher up the hill, Grandma shared her knowledge of the woods. Though she hadn't completed high school, she knew so much. She could identify scads of wildflowers—Dutchman's breeches, jack-in-the-pulpit, violets—and she knew the names of almost all the birds.

She showed us how to nip off the ends of honeysuckle blossoms, slowly draw out the pistils, and taste the sweet drop of nectar that clung to the tip. She held grasshoppers by their wings, saying, "Spit tobacco," and on command they would deposit a small drop of brown juice from their mouths onto her index finger. She could join small twigs into crosses or squares by peeling back some of the flexible green bark and using it as twine. She knotted clover blossoms into necklaces and draped them around our necks or tied them around our wrists.

When we passed the small brook that cascaded down the hill, she pointed to tadpoles wriggling across dark pools. She overturned rocks, revealing crayfish or slithering, spotted salamanders. Then she provided us with nature's Play-Doh. After scooping soft gray clay from under the falls, we molded it into figures of people or animals and set them out to dry in the sun.

But my grandmother taught me so much more. A serene, shy woman, who seemed to prefer the company of trees over that of people, Grandma often retreated to the woods, alone, to struggle with problems or just to think. She lived in communion with nature and seemed thoroughly at ease ambling along a wooded trail. By watching the ease that accompanied her into the woods, I learned to trust the wilderness while embracing its gifts.

We sometimes sat on rocks or downed logs for long minutes and looked down on the orderly rows of houses and streets in the distance. Or we just sat, listening to the cacophony of woodland sounds until sunlight waned and it was time to return to the house. My brother and I often made our descent by rolling down a long, gently sloping hillside covered with grass, and we arrived at the bottom giggling and dizzy, giddy from sheer joy.

Even as a writer, I find it difficult to explain how it felt to be in the woods with my grandmother. The feeling was so sublime, so serene, so personal. In the woods I found hope, peace, healing; no matter how sour my mood, the woods seemed always to soothe me, to resurrect sagging spirits. In the woods there was a sense of being at home, of being where I ought to have been all along.

Like my grandmother, I've often walked to the woods to think, to reflect, to sort things out. Even as an adolescent, when I en-countered difficult times, I sought the peace I knew I would find there. In high school, when my grandmother died, I instinctively followed my grief to the hill where I sat for an hour or more, look-ing, listening for an answer. And I believe I found it at the brook that, to this day, traces the clay banks down the hill, just as it did on my first visit years ago.

Years would pass before I learned about the Appalachian Trail in 1977, during the summer before my senior year in college. At the time, I was working on a landscaping crew, and one day during our lunch break, I sat in the cab of the truck with Jim Koegel, a quiet, intense man, four years my senior. A radio news program came on, and the announcer made some reference to the Appalachian Trail. Between bites of his sandwich, Jim mentioned he had hiked it the year before.

I had no idea where the trail was or where it went, so I probed him for information. He explained that the trail extended 2,100 miles from Maine to Georgia and that he had hiked it from end to end the summer before, starting in Georgia. At first I was incredu-lous: could a person really walk that far in one summer? Then

I pressed Jim for details, asking the same questions I would face dozens of times while on my hike: Was the way marked? What did he eat? Where did he sleep? Did he hike alone? Did he encounter wild animals? What did he do when it rained?

As the summer passed, I drew more and more information from Jim, not so much the information that pertained to logistics or miles, but more about the experiential value of his summer in the wilderness, how the trail had changed him, and what lessons it had taught. And I became ever more captivated by his varied experiences.

At the time, I was primed for a challenge. The years of my adolescence had been difficult ones, not just for me but for most of the men and women of my generation. To some extent, we had been shaped by the Vietnam War and all the events it had precipitated. During those years the country was rife with conflict and chaos.

Evenings, we watched the nightly news with out parents and saw corpses being dumped into body bags. We watched reports of the 1968 Democratic National Convention in Chicago, where Mayor Daley's police thrashed panic-stricken protestors. We heard our hard-line elders denigrate the unpatriotic hippies and peaceniks who protested the war. Meanwhile, race riots ripped the inner cities and in ways reached our snug, middle-class suburbs. I was surprised to learn from a friend that his father slept with a loaded shotgun under his bed.

Amid all the chaos there was excitement, and it penetrated every living room, every institution, every life. Everyone was full of passion, regardless of beliefs or convictions. So much was at stake. Men of draft age who had exhausted the deferment process faced war, prison, or escape to Canada. Blacks and other minorities faced continued oppression. And the establishment—middle-class Americans—feared an end to traditional values.

For those of us yet to come of age, there was a sense of an impending showdown. How would we respond when we received our draft notices? Would we go to war and earn the respect of our elders? Would we flee to Canada and face being disowned by our families? Would we be secure enough in our opposition to the war to accept a prison term by refusing to do either? Like most young men my age, I deferred the decision until I was forced to choose.

When I graduated from high school in 1974, I was eighteen and ready for the passage into adulthood, but by that time the matter had been rendered moot. The war was, in effect, over, and the government had begun pulling troops out of combat. The protests had ended. The commotion died. The era drew to a close. And everyone seemed badly in need of rest.

As the fury died, I was left feeling like a man who had spent years preparing—mentally, emotionally—for a test, only to arrive a day late to a darkened classroom and to realize that I would never know how well I might have done.

In the years following World War I, there emerged a generation of young Americans termed by Gertrude Stein, "the lost generation." It was a generation of restless young men and women, including Hemingway, Fitzgerald, T. S. Eliot, and others, who had fled America out of disgust or boredom to seek the excitement of Paris. Once there, the expatriates pursued a life of abandon—living, drinking, loving to excess—while trying to make sense of their world and times.

Then, after World War II, novelist Jack Kerouac chronicled the attitudes of a similar generation, the "beat generation," in his book *On the Road*.

It seems that there follows in the wake of war a pestering complacency that sends youthful seekers out in search of excitement and meaning. Those of us affected by Vietnam were no exception.

I won't go as far as to say that I envied my peers who has been born five years earlier, but at least they had been forced to examine their beliefs, to make decisions, and, once made, to put them to the test. I envied them the personal growth they had derived from being at the core of the revolution or in the heart of the battle.

But for me there was no war, no showdown. Instead, there was only college and a continuation of my comfortable life. Once in school, and without having made the slightest sacrifice, I savored all the privileges won by the young people who has preceded me and had waged the social revolution.

During my first year in college, the resident radicals who had orchestrated the college protests during the war years still appealed to the students to support one cause or another, but by that time they had begun to resemble caricatures of themselves. By the time I graduated in 1978, benign indifference had supplanted the zeal of the late sixties. Oxford-cloth shirts and khaki pants had replaced jeans and T-shirts, and the emphasis had shifted from pursuing spiritual, sensual, and political goals to securing high-paying jobs. The whole scene left me flat.

I graduated, fulfilling an obligation to my parents who had helped pay my way through college and expected me to finish. The rest of my life was my own, but I had no idea what I wanted to do with it. I only knew that I craved experience outside of the cozy environs that had sheltered me for the first twenty-three years of my life. I wanted to be challenged. I wanted to confront something new and different. I wanted to find out what I was made of.

Thanks to Jim Koegel, I knew just where to find such challenge. After hearing his tales of adventure in the eastern wilderness, I made the Appalachian Trail my quest. I had heard so many people lament lost dreams, things they had longed to do but never found the time for. I was determined to see that that didn't happen to me. The trail would pose a wonderful setting where I could live, as Thoreau expressed in *Walden*, simply and deliberately, with room to grow, to breathe, to change, to discover what really mattered to me.

In the end, the Appalachian Trail provided all those things and more. Like every one of the other several thousand or so end-to-enders who have hiked the trail since its completion in 1937, I emerged from the Maine woods transformed.

This book is a collection of experiences and encounters, stories of fear and courage, of risk, of friendship and intimacy, of the power and beauty of nature. For more than fifty years, the Appalachian Trail has offered footloose seekers a wooded path to spiritual and physical growth, to communion with the natural world, and to discovery of self. May it always continue to do so.

Acknowledgments

I would like to thank the following people for their support and encouragement while I hiked the Appalachian Trail and, later, while I wrote about it:

Dan, Nick, Paul, Victor, and Jimmy, and all the other backcountry travelers whose companionship has enriched my life.

My wife, Belinda, for her wisdom, kindness, and ever-nurturing way.

My daughters, Challen and Logan, who remind me always of what's important in this life.

My father, the first to read nearly everything I've ever written.

Giles Anderson, my agent, who does a wonderful job of managing the business end of writing.

Director Scot Danforth and my other friends at the University of Tennessee Press, who have deemed *As Far as the Eye Can See* worthy of yet another printing. And UT Press's Stephanie Thompson, who designed this edition's beautiful cover.

Brian King and the Appalachian Trail Conservancy, who have kept this book alive for more than two decades.

Steve Kemp, editor of *Smokies Life*, for nearly a decade of choice assignments that have led me along the trails of my favorite National Park.

Bill Lea, whose photo graces the cover of this edition and captures one of the finest mornings I've experienced in the mountains.

National Geographic Traveler editor-in-chief Keith Bellows, who offered me just the right advice as I stood at a career crossroads in 1987.

Ron Pitkin and Larry Stone, who took a chance on an unpublished book author 23 years ago.

CHAPTER ONE

Fear

I'm lying under a wind- and rain-buffeted tarp in a mountain gap in Georgia. I can hear wind gusts begin miles away, then gather intensity and plow through the gap, and, with each gust, the tarp sounds as if it's about to rip from its tethers. The trees creak, and I can hear limbs crack. I am terrified and awed by the power and violence of nature, and I realize that there's nowhere I can go to escape it. I never appreciated how vulnerable I'd feel away from the shelter of a roof and four sound walls.

APRIL 24, 1979
TESNATEE GAP, GEORGIA

 UST BEFORE A SPRING THUNDERSTORM HAMMERS the mountains, the animals disappear. The songbirds stop singing. The chipmunks stop scurrying. The spring peepers stop peeping. The crickets stop grinding. And quiet settles over the woods.

When twisters accompany those storms and rip their own random trails across the landscape, you nestle down in the deepest part of your sleeping bag and hope that your luck holds.

You also swear that you will never, ever camp in a mountain gap again. Tornados, like the pioneers of centuries past, often follow the gaps across mountain ranges. I know that now, but, on April 24,1979, as I lay under a nylon tarp in Tesnatee Gap, Georgia, I didn't.

There was, however, one thing that I knew for certain that night. I was frightened.

I had watched the storm approach from the west in the late hours of the afternoon. Columns of cumulo-nimbus clouds lumbered into view above the faraway hills, erasing the sun. The air smelled and felt pregnant with moisture, and, as the first winds began to buffet my camp, the atmosphere took on a sick, green cast.

By 6:00 p.m., it was dark, and I lay ensconced under my rain fly waiting, as the first peals of thunder rumbled a few miles away. I had learned that, by counting the seconds that lagged between each lightning flash and peal of thunder, I could estimate my distance from the heart of the storm. A five-second lag meant the storm was roughly one mile away. At 6:30 p.m., the storm was four miles away and approaching fast.

By 7:00 p.m., the counting game ended when the storm enveloped my camp. The ground rumbled beneath me, and the wind and rain raged above. I had experienced storms in the lowlands, secure inside four walls, but never in the mountains. At three thousand feet, I was wrapped in the low-slung clouds and, thus, inside the storm, and the thunder seemed to surround me before rolling away to the valleys.

Lightning bolts cast stark silhouettes of tree branches against the nylon of the tarp. First the flash, then, immediately after, the resounding crack of thunder, like the slow splintering of huge bones. Then there was the rain, which fell so heavily at times that the tarp sagged under its assault and brushed against my face, and I could hear torrents of water channeling downhill, carving away earth and stone.

The wind howled and churned like an errant locomotive and its force all but deadened the sound of the thunder and falling rain. I could hear walls of wind originate miles away in the valleys, then thrash toward me, gathering intensity as they approached. They plowed through the gap, bowing the trees, scattering leaves, and snapping limbs. As each passed, the rain fly popped and bucked and surged, and I feared that it would tear from its tethers and disappear into the darkness, leaving me exposed and even more vulnerable.

I cowered under the fly feeling utterly helpless, like a prairie dog trapped under the hooves of stampeding cattle, and I prayed for the storm to deliver me unharmed. Through the night, I felt like a victim, as if all the storm's violent energy had been directed at me and as if raw vengeance bolstered the wind and powered the rain. Though I wouldn't realize it until the next morning, a twister had already cut a swath through another gap a few miles to the north. I had been spared.

When day broke, I surveyed the damage wrought through the night. Tree trunks had been splintered, severed branches lay scattered about, and uprooted trees crisscrossed the trail with gray clay and stone still clinging to their dying roots.

At that point, I was four days and thirty-seven miles into the Appalachian Trail. I had begun my hike at Springer Mountain, the trail's southern terminus some sixty miles northeast of Atlanta, and I was determined to trek all the way to Mount Katahdin, the trail's northernmost point, in central Maine.

A month earlier, I had resigned my job as manager of a Washington, D.C., tennis shop and had committed myself and my meager $1,500 in savings to completing the trail. I wanted to become one of several hundred "thru-hikers" who had navigated the route from end to end in one summer, but other reasons, too, had drawn me toward the trail. Among them was the desire to confront and overcome my fears, but, in the wake of the storm, I realized that I had only begun to identify them. Moreover, I acknowledged that I couldn't hope to banish my fears until I had pushed deeper into the eastern wilderness and probed much farther into myself.

HOUGH FEAR IS A SOLITARY CONDITION, AT LEAST I had not had to endure the storm alone. I had shared my camp with Dan Howe, a twenty-three-year-old former architectural planner for a large oil corporation who had swapped his business suit and fast-track career for a pair of lug-soled boots, a backpack, and 2,100 miles of adventure. When we had set out on the trail, we had known each other just over a month and had met face to face only a half-dozen times.

Dan and I had first met during a program on the Appalachian Trail at a Washington-area backpacking shop. The program featured Ed Garvey, a well-known thru-hiker and author who had hiked the trail in the early 1970s. I had arrived for Garvey's talk fully reconciled to the notion that I would begin and finish the trail by myself, despite the fact that my previous backpacking experience had been limited to four or five overnighters; the longest duration had been three days. Over the previous months, I had telephoned every friend I had and even a few casual acquaintances, in hopes of cajoling one or more of them into taking up the trail with me.

Most of them, like me, were in their first year out of college but, unlike me, had devoted their energies to charting career paths rather than ambling along wilderness trails. While they regarded the Appalachian Trail as a romantic pursuit, they also recognized its potential for stalling a career climb, and, one by one, they declined my invitation. So, I had attended Garvey's presentation with the dim hope of finding a partner there.

As Garvey concluded his presentation, he asked if anyone among the thirty people in the audience intended to attempt the trail that summer. Tentatively, I raised my hand and then quickly scanned the room. One other hand waved in the air, and it belonged to a sandy-haired, bearded man who appeared to be about my age. After the meeting disbanded, I approached him and introduced myself, trying not to seem too eager or needy and realizing that to ask him abruptly if he would commit to spending the next five months with me was tantamount to proposing marriage on a first date.

Within a half-hour, Dan and I sat at a nearby tavern drinking beer and discussing our hopes, dreams, and expectations for our months on the trail. As we talked, I discovered that we had planned to begin the trail at about the same time—late April—and that we shared many common attitudes. Both of us had lived through the turbulent years of the late 1960s and early 1970s, and we both had emerged with a sense that, if society failed to provide the peace and stability we sought, we might find it in nature.

While I had begun the trail seeking nature's healing powers, over the first four days I had found only disappointment, discovering that nature was capable of more violence than I had ever experienced in civilization. I found disappointment, too, in discovering the fear that dwelt within me.

In the throes of the storm, I had lain awake, my heart thumping like that of a snared rabbit, while Dan slumbered peacefully beside me. Through the long night, my head churned a maelstrom of doubt and anxiety, and I began to suspect that I possessed neither the courage nor the stamina to reach Mount Katahdin, more than two thousand miles to the north. I also suspected that I had invested my hopes in a folly that would break me the way the wind had cracked away the branches of the surrounding trees and that I would limp back home wounded by failure. Those feelings may have been amplified by the storm, but they had just as surely accompanied my first tentative steps on the trail four days earlier.

ARLY ON THE MORNING OF APRIL 21, MY PARENTS had driven Dan and me up a ten-mile stretch of gravel road to Nimblewill Gap, which reaches within three miles of Springer Mountain and represents the nearest road access to the southern terminus of the Appalachian Trail.

An alternate route to the top follows an approach trail, which begins at Amicalola Falls State Park and ascends nine miles to

Springer. We had heard stories about the stiff, vertical ascent from the park to the trailhead, reputed to be among the trail's most difficult sections. This was especially the case for neophyte hikers who lacked the fitness and stamina that hundreds of miles on the trail would later provide. Among the dozens of hopeful thru-hikers who abandon the trail each year, in fact, many stumble back down the mountain—defeated—before ever reaching the summit of Springer. We didn't want to be among them, and, by starting our hike at Nimblewill, we reasoned, we would at least make it as far as the official starting point.

We arrived at the gap in my parents' new sedan, and Dan and I climbed from the car smelling of soap and shampoo, fresh from our last hot shower for many days. Once out of the car, Dan, a seasoned woodsman who had logged countless miles on backcountry trails, hefted his pack from the trunk and slid effortlessly into its straps. The process wasn't quite as easy for me.

First, there was the actual heft of my pack. I realize now that there is no more reliable method for gauging a hiker's confidence than studying the contents of his pack. The least experienced hikers labor under a yoke of fear and worry, cluttering their packs with devices they hope will duplicate the security of more familiar environments. Veteran hikers, whose packs are characteristically spartan, have discovered that a well chosen poem or quotation, which weighs nothing once committed to memory, can provide more solace in the face of fear than a welter of gadgets and trinkets.

Since I was a novice, my backpack burgeoned with expendable items that catered either to my fears or to my vanity but which served no purpose other than to occupy space with their bulk and stress my knees with their weight. While Dan's pack weighed a respectable thirty-five to forty pounds, mine surpassed fifty-five. I had read and reread backpacking how-to books, which sang the praises of lightweight packs bearing only the essentials. In the months before the outset of my hike, I had loaded the pack dozens of times, and each time I tried to assess honestly the merit of each item I slipped into the pockets. Gradually, I had pared the pack down to forty pounds. As the day of departure approached, however, my doubts and fears reversed the trend, and I found myself sneaking small items back into the pack until the scales again topped fifty-five.

On the eve of the hike, I had down-loaded the pack one last time, and I resolved to leave it just as it was. To assuage my fears, though, I had stashed the discarded items in the trunk of the car. As I wrestled the pack onto the ground in Nimblewill Gap and glimpsed them for the last time, each suddenly seemed essential, and I realized that, once the trunk was closed, I would be forced to live without them.

Wouldn't the two-pound pair of binoculars in their leather case bring me closer to wildlife and help me identify the denizens of my new environment? Wouldn't the plastic egg-carrier and fifty feet of braided marine rope prove indispensable? What about the extra cook pot, aluminum plate, and oven mitt? Would one pair of long trousers be enough, and did I need a third pair of wool socks? Would the sheath knife, with its six-inch blade, protect me from wild beasts, or would my Swiss Army knife be sufficient? Would the package of firecrackers and can of dog repellent chase marauding bears from our camps? Would the metal pocket mirror, which doubled as a signal mirror, become an invaluable grooming aid or even save my life if I became lost? Wouldn't the one-pound hammock help make my leisure hours more comfortable? Would my health fail without the three-month supply of vitamins and the bulky first-aid manual?

As I deliberated, Dan shifted impatiently, and I resolved finally that the egg-carrier, binoculars, oven mitt, sheath knife, and marine rope would stay behind. The mirror, the first-aid guide, the firecrackers, the hammock, the extra pair of socks and trousers, the supplemental pot and plate, the vitamins, and dog repellent, I reasoned, would justify their weight.

At the time, my pack, as heavy as it was, seemed far less burdensome than the emotional and physical challenge that awaited me, and, as I glimpsed the trailhead, I first registered the full impact of what I was about to do. I had been raised by conservative and protective parents, who tended not to venture far from the cloister of their snug, middle-class environment. From the time I was young, my life had been predicated on safe decisions. Now, I was about to embark on a five-month journey through the unknown, where I would face risks more real than any I had known before.

Fueling my fears was the knowledge that, once I entered the backcountry, I would leave behind the familiar trappings of the civilized world—electric lights to chase away the darkness, television sets and radios to help fill the idle hours, modern appliances to ease the chores of daily life—and the comfort they provided. I had fully enjoyed the morning's hot shower and the meal at the hotel restaurant. I felt no shame in ascending into the mountains inside the climate-controlled environment of the car, and I wasn't at all sure I could endure life without those and other amenities.

In some ways, the act of climbing from the car was tantamount to exiting the womb: I faced a strange and forbidding new world. At least in the first instance I had been blessed with conscientious parents who shepherded me clear of major pitfalls. Once I entered the woods, I knew that there would be nothing to shield me from hardship and danger except my own resources, which I had never really tested.

When the time to leave came, I embraced my parents and hoped they would offer some advice or guidance, yet I realized that I was about to enter a realm they knew little about.

"Be careful," said my mother, with tears welling in her eyes.

"Yes, and have fun," Dad advised, as I took the first of the five million steps that would lead me to Mount Katahdin. After a few hundred feet, I turned one last time to see the white sedan disappear in a cloud of dust as it descended the gravel road. For the first time in my life, I was truly on my own.

Within an hour and a half, we reached Springer, a rounded mountain cloaked in hardwood trees, their branches tipped with opening buds, and we discovered a sign-in book wedged into a mailbox planted on the summit. We took the register to a grassy clearing and basked for a few minutes in the eighty-two-degree sunshine as we read the entries logged by other hikers who had begun the hike in previous days and weeks. Dan and I noted that eight hikers, all bound for Maine, had signed in over the weekend, and we were two of the nearly five hundred who would set out on the northward pilgrimage that summer. At that point, none of us knew who would be among the one hundred or so who would reach our goal.

I penned a brief message about my dream of reaching Katahdin and then signed my name. Under it I drafted the thru-hiker symbol: a capital T nestled under and joined with the crossbar of a capital A. Beside it, I printed the letters GA, the designation for Georgia, with an arrow pointing to the letters ME, the abbreviation for Maine, and added the year: 1979. In so doing, I became an official Appalachian Trail thru-hiker.

Before continuing north, Dan and I posed for pictures beside a forest service sign. It listed Springer Mountain and its elevation of 3,782 feet along with the distance to a few major mileposts ahead. The last entry was Mount Katahdin, mileage two thousand miles (since the sign had been erected, trail relocations had added about one hundred miles). From the perspective of the wooded hills of Georgia at the base of the Appalachian spine, the northern terminus wouldn't have seemed more remote if it had been located on the surface of the moon.

For the next several days, we traversed the three-thousand-foot peaks of the Chattahoochee National Forest. I count those days among the most difficult I have endured. I spent most of them absorbed in the rigors of survival in an environment that seemed foreign and hostile. In short, I was consumed by apprehension and fear.

I was afraid of my own ineptitude. I fumbled with my new stove, lost track of items stored in my pack, and listened at night as mice gnawed through my foodbag, before I learned to hang it out of their reach. I had no idea how to bushwhack down a mountainside to locate a water source, what to do to protect myself on an exposed ridge in a thunderstorm, how to patch myself back together after

I had sliced myself with my pocket knife, how long to boil lentils and rice, how much stove fuel to carry for the days and nights between supply stops, and how much and what type of food I would need to keep from starving.

I was afraid of my own weakness. My lungs burned, my thighs ached, and my feet throbbed as my boots rubbed my tender heels to blisters on the first few steep ascents, and I wondered if I had the fortitude to keep pushing on through the pain. When late April storms drenched the woods, I dreaded leaving the dry warmth of my shelter to set out for fifteen miles through the downpour. I was afraid, too, of facing my friends back home if I failed to meet those challenges and had to pack it in.

I was afraid of being alone. Dan's woods-sense far exceeded my own, and I stuck by him like moss on a log, worried that if I let him out of my sight, I would never catch up to him and would be left to earn my proficiency through hardship and failure. As it turned out, Dan taught me much, and we remained a team to the very pinnacle of Mount Katahdin. During our five months on the trail, we propped each other up when our spirits flagged, fought like badgers when our egos pulled in different directions, and shared our food, our shelter, and our thoughts. When the trip ended, we had spent more than 150 days and nights together and had forged a friendship that will endure no matter how much time and distance separate us.

I was afraid of the vast mystery of nature. The chilling echo of hoot owls, the distant drumming of male ruffed grouse beating the air with their wings, and the constant rustling in the brush around our camps after we'd extinguished our evening campfires were all unfamiliar sounds that fueled my fear.

And, I was afraid when, under a tarp in Tesnatee Gap, I first experienced the raw power of nature.

The fear inspired by that first spring storm—and all the fears that accompanied me along my first miles on the trail—soon fused into a pervading sense of dread. As I watched Dan confront the trail's challenges with courage and confidence, I began to resign myself to the belief that I wasn't quite suited for an extended stay

AS FAR AS THE EYE CAN SEE

in the woods. One evening, while I sat on a log, downcast and preparing to tell him that I had decided to leave the trail, a toy collie strayed into camp. Though I didn't realize it at the time, I was about to learn the first, and perhaps the most enduring, lesson about life on the trail. Put simply, if one is receptive and open to change, the trail—and in a larger sense, nature itself—seems always to answer one's questions and meet one's needs. It sounds mystical, and I wouldn't believe it if I hadn't experienced it so many times along my journey.

Just behind the dog, a woman in her late fifties labored up the trail, the huge pack she carried dwarfing her slight frame. Her legs appeared much too frail to support her own weight, much less the weight of the pack, and her face, framed by silver shoulder-length hair, registered the pain of every step.

She paused for a few minutes, leaning on her walking stick, and told us that her name was Elizabeth and that she was hiking alone. Her destination, like ours, was Mount Katahdin. She told us that her husband had died the previous year and that she had taken up the trail to ease her grief and to chart a new direction for her life. She said she covered twelve to fifteen miles per day, beginning at dawn and continuing until dark.

She declined our invitation to join us in our camp, saying that she hoped to cover a few more miles before it became too dark to navigate the boulder-strewn trail. Soon, she called to her dog and resumed her slow, deliberate pace.

Later, as Dan and I sat beside the fire plotting our mileage for the next several days and as I struggled with the decision to continue on or abandon the trail, I couldn't shake the memory of Elizabeth. It had taken me five hours to cover the twelve miles to camp that day; she had been plodding along for nearly twice that long. At the end of each day, my twenty-three-year-old thighs and feet ached. How then must hers have felt? I had shuddered as the storm blew through our camp, and I had flinched in the darkness when the trees creaked and wild animals crept unseen through the underbrush. Yet, I had the comfort of a companion. How did she contend with such fears during her solitary days and nights on the trail? How had she become so brave?

Frankly, in spite of her apparent courage, I had dismissed Elizabeth's goal of completing the trail as foolhardy. Yet, one evening some five months later, while Dan and I camped in the woods of central Maine, a toy collie entered camp. As soon as we saw it, we looked at one another and smiled. Then, we turned and looked up the trail. A slender figure soon emerged from the trees. It was Elizabeth.

Although the previous five months had wrought physical changes in all of us, the rigors of trail life had completely transformed Elizabeth. Her face was wan and haggard, and dark circles had formed under her eyes. Her legs seemed to have lost what little muscle tone they had had, and her silver hair had billowed into a tangled mass. Her gait seemed even more painful and unsteady than when I had first seen her.

Once she joined us in camp, she explained that she had made it as far as New England before realizing that, at her pace, she could not hope to reach Katahdin before the end of October, when Baxter State Park officials bar access to the mountain because of unpredictable weather. She had decided to "flop," as do many of the slower-moving hikers, and travel to Katahdin, then hike south to where she had left off. I later learned that she reached her goal.

When I refer back to my journal entry on the night we first met Elizabeth in Georgia, I find a message of hope. There, I termed her "Our Lady of the Trail" and wrote that "she seems weak and distant and unaware of the difficulty of the task that awaits her. We have heard about other hikers who have already gotten discouraged and gone home. But, after these few days, she is still here, still moving north. How, I don't know. She will always be an inspiration to me."

Thereafter, Elizabeth became my guiding spirit, like a figurehead on an old wooden ship leading frightened sailors through uncharted seas. When my confidence began to fail, I would think of her and her frail body facing the wilderness alone with no one to ease her fears or share her discoveries. From then on, I resolved that, although I could not conquer my fears outright, I could at least confront them squarely. As I did, they seemed to lose their power over me.

As the weeks passed, my blisters began to heal, and my thighs grew hard and strong. My camp routine became well enough ingrained that I could fetch water, fire the stove, cook and eat dinner, and hang my food without a wasted motion. My pack and its contents became more familiar to me than my dresser drawers at home, and I eventually discarded the spare socks, extra cook pot and plate, vitamins, firecrackers, dog repellent, and several other pounds of extraneous gear. I gave the extra trousers to a fellow hiker who had ripped the seat out of his own, and soon my pack dipped to a manageable thirty-five pounds.

From then on, I carried only the essentials. As the load in my pack decreased, my initial fear of the wilderness mellowed, and I began walking my fifteen to twenty miles each day alone, fascinated with the process of spring awakening around me. I even began to regard thunderstorms, which weeks earlier had pitched me into panic, as among nature's most formidable and entertaining displays, more potent and grand than anything I had witnessed in civilization. Many evenings, as storms approached, I scrambled to an open perch on a ridge-line from which to watch them, as their charcoal-gray sentries floated across dusky skies stretching to the horizon. I sat captivated as their silver talons raked nearby mountain peaks and their thunder shook the earth. As I watched, I began to realize that my transformation from visitor to resident of the wilderness had begun and that there was much yet to learn about my new home.

CHAPTER TWO

Learning to Walk, Learning to See

This lifestyle certainly allows plenty of time for introspection. Most days, I spend six or seven hours alone, walking, out of sight and sound of any other human being. Some days, my thoughts turn inward, and I pass the miles exploring memories of people and events that have shaped my past. Other days, my mind nestles into a meditative daze, and I sense myself connected to the birds, the plants, the flowers, the trees, like a man floating on the breeze through a boundless garden.

MAY 29, 1979
IRON MOUNTAIN SHELTER, TENNESSEE

E OFTEN DEFINE OURSELVES BY OUR PRIMARY OCCUPA-tions. A person who busies himself painting houses, for instance, is a painter. A person who devotes his energies to growing crops is a farmer. In that sense, during my months on the Appalachian Trail, I was a hiker, and the simple act of hiking—lifting each boot, planting it squarely, and biting off

another three-foot section of trail—came to define who I was.

Though simple in terms of mechanics, hiking proved to be a complex process that evolved over time into an almost meditative act that touched me daily in physical and spiritual ways. But, before I could savor the more sublime virtues of hiking, I had to submit to an often demanding apprenticeship, one that I undertook at the heels of my hiking companion, Dan.

There was a grace inherent in Dan's gait, and I detected it the first time we hiked together. On our first shakedown hike, a two-day trip to the Shenandoah National Park, we covered fifteen miles under a constant downpour. During the first day, I watched in awe as Dan approached a rain-swollen stream, leapt from the ground onto a downed tree spanning the creek, and crossed without breaking stride. The tree was maybe six inches in diameter and had been stripped of its bark, making it as slick as a greased iron post. The murky stream had spilled over its banks and roared beneath. Adding to the challenge were the hard-rubber soles of our hiking boots, which provided precarious footing at best on a wet surface. Nonetheless, Dan ambled across the log as surely as if he were traversing a flat dirt path wearing baseball spikes, and, once on the other side, he stopped to watch me make my pass.

I eased onto the log, feeling my muscles tighten, and, after taking two unsteady steps, with my arms and legs tracing hula hoops in the air, I plunged waist-deep into the stream. Dragging myself up the far bank, I unleashed a string of expletives as Dan, laughing, disappeared up the trail. That night, while I slumbered restlessly in the tent, I had a dream that fashioned my frustration into a metaphor.

In the dream, I awoke in the darkness and found myself clinging to a life raft that was being dragged through rough seas at high speed. As the foam spattered my face, I spied through the darkness a long rope tethered to the raft and leading a few hundred yards forward to the stern of a huge cruise ship. The ship was kicking up a fearful wake, and I could see Dan standing aboard ship and peering at me from the deck.

I didn't require an analyst to interpret the dream. I obviously was worried that I would never match Dan's speed or agility, and I saw myself forever in the wash, slogging along the trail in wet boots and sodden clothes, careening into every stream and tumbling over every obstacle. What I failed to realize at the time was that the problems I encountered did not reflect any in-born lack of balance or coordination. Rather, they lay in my inexperience, which made me regard the pack as an accessory rather than an extension of my physical self.

Once on the trail in April, I underwent a period of adjustment during which I gradually learned to accommodate the load on my back through subtle shifts in muscles and balance. Actually, the change took place unconsciously, much the way a mail carrier might gradually lean in one direction to offset the weight of the mailbag. It would be weeks, however, before I had accomplished the necessary changes and could stride surely across such obstacles as fallen logs. Eventually, the pack became a part of me, and I soon felt only partially clothed without it.

Once I had adapted to the pack, I began to experience the opposite problem and discovered that my balance wavered when I took it off at the end of a long day. I wasn't alone in that regard. I recall watching many of my fellow hikers arrive in camp and, once relieved of their loads, stumble like drunken men.

Balance was one component of hiking; strength and endurance were others. During our first days on the trail, the twelve- and thirteen-mile days seemed interminable, and, as each day passed, I grimaced as I glanced up the trail and beheld yet another ascent lurking ahead. The trail seemed to be a never-ending continuum of ascents that taxed my thighs and descents that stressed my knees, with hardly a flat quarter-mile stretch to ease the twitching in my fatigued muscles.

At the same time, I suffered a pestering preoccupation with distance, how much mileage I had covered through each day and how much remained ahead until I would reach camp. I even wore a pedometer attached to my belt to measure my progress by the length of my stride. It worked, in a sense, but, by wearing it, I became like the motorist who fixes on the odometer while excluding the scenery rolling past. Like such a motorist, I never seemed to draw much closer to my destination.

Beyond my daily mileage, there was the larger perspective—the distance to the northern terminus of the trail—and I found myself constantly subtracting the miles I had covered from the total to Mount Katahdin. Even at the time, that struck me as ludicrous, like counting every chisel stroke invested in carving the presidents' heads into Mount Rushmore, and it imparted little sense of motion. Such a means of gauging my progress—focusing on the remaining miles to the trail's end rather than taking each day in turn—reminded me of a line from T.S. Eliot's poem, "The Love Song of J. Alfred Prufrock," about a man who ponders his misspent life and concludes, sadly, that he's measured out his life "with coffee spoons." Prufrock had his coffee spoon; I had my pedometer.

Thru-hiking was not, after all, a race, though some hikers seemed inclined to view it as one. Over the summer, each of the dozens of thru-hikers I met seemed to fall into one of two categories. First were those intent on savoring the trail experience, while still viewing Katahdin as the ultimate goal. They tended to measure the miles in terms of quality—of events and experience— rather than quantity. These were the hikers who, I believe, learned and grew the most while on the trail. Most of my colleagues fell into this camp. Shortly after discarding my pedometer, I joined their ranks.

There were others—the peak-baggers—who viewed completing the Appalachian Trail as a Spartan feat that would enhance their sense of machismo without reconfiguring their attitudes or values. To many of them, the trail became an ultraendurance footrace that, once completed, would provide another certificate to hang on their walls and another patch to sew onto their backpacks. Covering the 2,100 miles with their hearts and minds fixed on the final peak, they missed the important peaks that led to it.

Among us were men and women who embodied the extremes of each philosophy. There were, for instance, hikers who dallied too long in trail towns or who sacrificed too many days by refusing to walk in the rain. In the end, completion of the trail eluded them. I recall a pair of hikers from New Jersey who hiked when they felt like it and lounged around in camp or hitchhiked into town when they didn't. Most of the time, they didn't, and, as far as I know, they never reached Katahdin.

There were others who dallied not at all and dashed up the trail as if pursued by demons. Late one evening in a shelter near Erwin, Tennessee, for instance, a hiker arrived in the dark, at 9:30 p.m. After a hasty greeting, he munched a few handfuls of dry trail mix, unrolled his bag, slept until 5:30 a.m., munched a few more handfuls of Good Old Raisins and Peanuts (GORP), and hit the trail by 5:45. As he ate, I propped myself on one elbow, disinclined to leave the warmth of my sleeping bag, and asked him a few questions.

I discovered that he had less than three months to finish the trail before he had to return to school, and he covered twenty-five to thirty miles each day. What's more, he had not taken a day off since he had left Springer and was fully reconciled to the fact that his entire summer might pass without a single idle day to laze around town or wallow in a mountain lake. As I listened, he outlined his schedule for the next several weeks: Harpers Ferry by this date, the White Mountains by another, and Katahdin by another, leaving him less than a week to digest the trail experience, return home, gather his books, and return to school. The schedule could not have been more oppressive if it had belonged to an overworked corporate executive.

Another such hiker, George, a Massachusetts native known as Pigpen because of his stolid refusal to bathe, had secured a four-month leave of absence from his accounting firm in Boston. The leave left him just enough time to finish the trail, barring any unexpected problems. I hiked with George for several days in Georgia and North Carolina before he blasted ahead under the strain of his deadline.

I learned later that, once George reached New England, the trail had worked its magic, and his priorities had shifted. The threat of losing his job and his single-minded determination to reach Mount Katahdin, which had propelled him ahead at his furious pace, suddenly seemed to contradict the essence of the trail experience, that it's the journey itself, not the journey's end, that offers the greatest reward. George finally called his boss, asked for and received an extension, finished the trail, and eventually returned to the office. The last I heard, he was considering chucking both his navy-blue suits and his job to take up long-distance cycling.

By late May, the trail had begun to affect me, too, and I began to view my daily mileage as a wholesome addiction. I had reached a level of physical stamina that I had not known before and have never achieved since, and each day's end found me feeling energized, cleansed, and relaxed, with endorphins (the body's natural opiates released by exercise) coursing through my system. I soon settled into a constant three-mile-an-hour pace, no faster or slower than that of my fellow hikers, Dan included. The pace seldom varied, whether I was climbing or descending, unless, of course, I decided to throttle back to take in a view or study the flowers lining the trail.

I had come to relish hiking and the feeling of physical prowess that accompanied it, but it wasn't until the day in late May when we ascended Roan Mountain, a hulking six-thousand-footer in northeastern Tennessee, that I first experienced the sheer bliss of foot travel. The ascent to the top led up two thousand vertical feet, which would have destroyed me a month earlier. A freak snowstorm had blown in the previous day, layering the entire wilderness in a crystal glaze, and I remember the climb as a continuum of fairytale scenes and vistas: the surrounding snow-clad peaks, pink rhododendron and delicate mountain laurel blossoms frozen in full flower, and ice-laden spruce boughs shimmering in the sun. Along the steep ascent, utter fascination supplanted any concern I might have had over distance or altitude. As I reached the open, sun-drenched alpine meadows at the top, I realized that I would gladly have scaled four thousand more feet just for the opportunity to see it.

After the ascent, I realized how effortless climbing could be if one simply let the muscles and lungs work while savoring the beauty of each mile in its turn. Hiking soon evolved into a meditative act. There was euphony in the measured, purposeful sound of motion: the rhythmic rise and fall of breath, the thump of the heart, the cadence of boots crunching soil and rock, the steady tap of the walking stick, the bending of knees, and the flexing and relaxing of thigh muscles, calf muscles, hip muscles.

There were days when I focused on the scenery and I ambled along the trail feeling connected to the birds, plants, flowers, and trees, like a man floating on the breeze through a boundless garden. There were other days when the trees melded into two green labyrinthine walls that contained and guided me, and my mind traced other trails, scattered with people and events drawn from my past.

Memories I had lost or forgotten seemed to surface of their own accord, bringing with them vivid images, sensations, emotions, and voices, and I spent hours in their company. I relived my first date—with a shy brunette—in eighth grade; I embraced my high-school lover in the back seat of my old blue Impala; I circled the bases as a Little Leaguer after hitting my first and only grand-slam home run; I sparred with a high school rival at a Friday-night dance over the affections of a young woman; I relived the long summer afternoons as a child with my grandmother, exploring the woods and identifying wildflowers; and I relived the night my father entered my bedroom and, crying, told me she was dead.

And so—lost in thought—I passed the miles, and often, by day's end, I was jarred from my reverie by the sound of companions ahead in camp. I would then realize that I had traveled six or ten or twelve miles without recalling a single step.

I began to notice, too, how changes in the weather conjured up different moods. When gentle rains came, the woods swirled with mist, the leaves drooped, the ground became sodden brown, and the air hung rich with the smells of damp humus and musky ferns. On rain days, I cinched my parka hood around my face and drew within, enshrouded in the same clouds that swallowed the treetops and muted vibrant colors to hues of brown and gray.

Rain days were quiet days, with the hiss of a million drops plinking the palms of leaves and drowning the sounds of birds and wind and even the cadence of my boots. Often during such days, I delved into the repertoire of poems I had memorized since grade school—poems by Frost, Coleridge, Yeats, Kipling—and recited them aloud as I hiked, confident that no one could hear.

Or, I bellowed lyrics of favorite songs into the indifferent face of the rain and fog. One of them, "Taxi," a Harry Chapin song, always seemed to fit the mood of the rain: "It was raining hard in Frisco; I needed one more fare to make my night. . . ." The song, about a taxi driver who encounters his former lover on a dismal night, seemed doubly tragic in the rain, and I was moved by the pang of sadness it aroused.

On the other hand, sunny days were expansive days, especially when the trail snaked across bald-topped mountains or over exposed rock ledges where one's perspective was as broad as the horizon. Spence Field, in the southern section of the Great Smoky Mountains National Park, offered such a view, and we lazed for an hour or more in the grassy meadows there, tracing the mountains to where they yielded to the foothills and beyond to where the hills gave way to the plains and farther still to where long-fingered TVA lakes probed into hidden coves.

F MY EXPERIENCES DURING MY FIRST WEEKS ON THE trail taught me a new way to walk, they also provided me with a new way to see. Much as a novice audiophile might fail to appreciate the subtle qualities—tempo, pitch, melody, harmony—hidden in a musical composition, I, too, failed to notice many of the woods' subtle offerings before I had developed a sensitivity to the sounds, rhythms, and sights of the wilderness. There were baldfaced hornets' nests hanging in branches; songbirds flitting among the leaves; lizards and snakes slithering across sunbaked rocks; ground-hogs burrowing among fallen leaves; hawks and buzzards circling on thermals; bears nestling in treetops. And, there was spring in the Appalachians. Each day as the frail-green phalanx of opening buds crept up the mountains, the trail revealed new secrets.

CHAPTER THREE

Seasons

The colors of the leaves are incredible! In just the past few days, they have broken into full fall color. Reds and oranges predominate in the lowlands, and dark evergreens contrast with yellow birches on the mountain tops. The foliage should be at its peak when we climb Katahdin within a week, and we're all grateful for the perfect timing. The arrival of fall marks the fourth season we've walked through, completing the cycle. When we began in April, winter clung to the upper elevations as spring began its slow ascent. Then, summer overtook spring. Fall, like winter, takes the opposite route, beginning at the mountain tops and working its way down the slopes, sparking summer green to fire as it advances.

There is no describing the hiker's-eye-view of the changing seasons and living the continuous transition day by day, hour by hour.

SEPTEMBER 22, 1979
COOPER BROOK FALLS LEAN-TO, MAINE

VEN TODAY—MORE THAN TWENTY-FIVE YEARS AFTER I completed the trail—I suffer pangs of nostalgia with spring's onset. When those first spring days arrive and the whole world seems charged with passion and energy, I sit at a traffic light, bound for work in my climate-controlled office, and roll down my windows to savor the spring air, fragrant with the aroma of a million blossoms. I eye the landscaper, the carpenter, the maintenance worker seated in the truck beside me. I see him clad in work clothes, with the first ruddy traces of sun coloring his cheeks, and I envy him for his days spent outside and his intimacy with the seasons.

I realize that I, with my desk job, will witness the spring in scattered glimpses, while paused at traffic lights, at lunch hours spent on park benches, on weekends spent tilling my garden. And, I realize, sadly, that one day the spring will have passed, and it will be summer, and I will remind myself, as I always do, to pay closer attention next year. But, I seem never to succeed at it; too many things distract me. At such times, I fondly remember my journey through the Appalachians where, in my memory, it is always spring.

The trail forever changed my perspective on the seasons. On the trail, I *lived* the seasons. I experienced them moment to moment, sensing one season's gradual surrender to the next. There was no urgency, just the perennial cycle of death and life played out in slow fluid motion, every morning providing new evidence of change.

First, there was winter, gripping the higher elevations where barren limbs rattled in icy winds and where everything was dormant brown except the green conifers, the clusters of shiny galax, and the scatterings of aromatic wintergreen. Meanwhile, at the lower elevations, spring's most resilient sprigs probed through layers of decaying foliage and buds burst open on deciduous trees. A phalanx of frail green marked the place where the two seasons met.

I remember the first time I saw it. I had ascended Albert Mountain, a boulder-strewn nob topped with a fire tower in North

Carolina, one hundred miles north of Springer Mountain. It was April 29, and, as I looked out across the surrounding ridges and valleys, first I saw the deep-green swatches of fir trees. Then, I noted the barren mountain crests. Far below were lowlands tinged in green. Between, an asymmetric line of the faintest green traced the boundary between death and life, between winter and spring. If someone were to have asked me at that moment where and when spring arrived, I could have provided an answer. Pointing to that line, I would have said, "There, this very minute, along that faint green line, spring is overtaking winter." And, if we had paused long enough and were patient enough, we could have watched it move. Naturalists claim that the line ascends at a rate of six feet per day, three inches every hour.

As we traced the line of the ridges and dipped into saddles and sags on our way north, we crossed that boundary countless times. As the days passed, the last vestiges of winter retreated higher and higher up the mountains until finally, by June, spring had surmounted even the six-thousand-foot peaks. Meanwhile, deep in the valleys, summer awakened and began its own slow ascent.

There was so much to see in the spring; every parcel of trail presented a colorful floral display. Dan carried a wildflower identification book in his pack, and, evenings in camp, he reported his latest findings. Together, we learned to call each flower by its rightful name.

There were delicate bluets, their four lavender lobes emerging from a golden, star-burst center and their needle-thin stems rising out of trailside grass. Wild irises, their rigid spiked leaves deep green and their blossoms curled like lips into a rich purple kiss. Jack-in-the-pulpits, with their green mottled leaves curled around and over a phallic spadix, a legion of upright preachers ministering to the emerging vegetation of the season's fertile rite. Lady's-slippers, with their soft pink labia transmitting a similar, though more delicate, message. Trilliums—pink ones, yellow ones, purple ones, striped ones—with their trilobed heads and leaves nourished beside rotting logs.

Bloodroot, with its variegated leaves, shaped as if by elfin scissors, sheltering a shy white flower. Buttercups, with tiny, waxen, gold pedals. Yellow and purple violets. Mayapples, with tight-wrapped leaves slowly swirling open like green picnic umbrellas, shading a round, white flower. Flame azalea trees, burning like fire with bright orange blossoms visible from hundreds of yards away. Fiddlehead ferns, uncoiling like cobras along the trail. Dutchman's breeches, with white blossoms dangling from a pale bowed spike, like tiny trousers hung on a line to dry. Showy orchids, a two-tone blending of violet and pure white. And the dogwoods decked in white and pink.

As the forest floor began to teem with flowers, the birds also awakened. Scarlet tanagers lit in dogwood trees, lending their red plumage to the bouquet of white blossoms. The brown wood thrush, with its auburn head, brown wings, and brown-spotted belly, trilled its lyrical flute-like song, of which Thoreau wrote, "Whenever a man hears it he is young, and nature is in its spring." Pileated woodpeckers, with their oversized, tufted red heads and narrow necks, screeched through the woods like winged banshees. Indigo buntings glowed iridescent purple in the sunlight. Chick-adees, tufted titmice, and rufous-sided towhees seemed to inhabit every tree and bush. Hoot owls' eerie four-syllable calls echoed through the trees around our camps, and we joked that they were really saying, "Whooo cooks for yooooo?"

And then there were the whip-poor-wills that irked us through many nights with their frenetic calls, beginning their arias about the time we climbed into our bags and often continuing until dawn. We frequently lobbed rocks in their direction but never scored a direct hit. More often than not, our mortars seemed only to intensify their maddening songs.

By late June, the spring buds had given way to the first of summer's flowering plants. Softball-sized rhododendron blossoms, ranging from rose-red to pink-white, exploded in such profusion that they washed entire mountainsides with their color. Mountain laurel, with its white, star-shaped blossoms punctuated with ten rosy dots, offered itself to us from bushes that draped over the trail. Pink musk thistle, white daisies, and golden black-eyed susans bowed to summer breezes in open fields and along country roads. Turk's-cap lilies, their knifelike petals curled into spotted orange turbans, grew as tall as seven feet and peered down on us as we traversed ridgeline trails through Virginia. Firepink and Indian paintbrush advertised their presence along the trailside with neon-red, dime-sized blossoms.

The bounty of edible plants and berries enhanced the beauty of the forest in bloom. Ramps, wild leeks with drooping, green, rabbit-ear leaves, thrived along the trail in Georgia, North Carolina, and Tennessee. The Indians used the plant's essence to treat insect bites; hikers use the bulbs and leaves to add garlic tang to soups and stews.

We had been searching for ramps for days after encountering a mountain woman, clad in a gingham dress and carrying a woven basket, who scoured the trail for ramps, wild mushrooms, and edible snails brought out by spring rains. She had shown us a ramp and slit open the bulb with her thumbnail, inviting us to sniff. The aroma brought tears, and we reasoned that anything with such a potent smell would pose an easy quarry. We were mistaken, and, after plucking from the loam dozens of trout lilies, which also boast drooping green leaves but no tang, we were ready to abandon hope. Then, as we passed through Beech Gap three miles north of the summit of Standing Indian Mountain, I spotted a trio of green leaves and determined to make one last try. I tugged on the leaves, which snapped off in my hands, and realized I had found our illusive ramp as the odor of garlic filled my nostrils.

That night, camped at the Carter Gap Shelter, we had a ramp-fest, slicing, dicing, and chopping the leaves and bulbs and dropping handfuls into our evening stews. One of our more daring colleagues, who experimented by eating an entire bulb raw, soon sat weeping over his cook pot, a beatific grin spreading across his tear-stained face.

Unfortunately, while the mountain woman had cited the culinary virtues of ramps, she had said nothing about their disastrous side effects. The morning after our ramp orgy, the shelter reeked, in spite of its open face. Well into the next day, acrid ramp burps curled my tongue, and I would have parted with my sleeping bag and pack for a single roll of antacid tablets. As my stomach churned, I swore off ramps, vowing to starve before I ever sampled another bulb. Unfortunately, my hiking buddies were not so inclined, and they continued to spice their evening meals with ramps until the leaves toughened later in the season and the plant sprouted a cluster of white flowers.

I soon learned that, although eating ramps is pure bliss for the strong of stomach, for the abstainer, living alongside anyone who has eaten them is pure hell. The pungent aroma not only stays on the breath but is exuded through the skin, taints the sweat, and lingers on clothing for days afterward.

Fortunately, most of nature's bounty was more sweet than acid. The same woman who had helped us identify ramps also showed us lemon balm, a member of the mint family with a square stalk, reddish-green variegated leaves, and a tart, lemony smell. We steeped the leaves in boiling water, added honey, and drank lemon-balm tea.

Near Hot Springs, North Carolina, thirty-five miles north of the Smokies, a toothless wanderer who shared our camp disappeared at dusk and returned with an armload of poke, a green edible weed with poison roots and dark red-blue berries later in the season. He boiled the leaves, dumped the water, and boiled them again. Once done, he smothered the leaves in butter from a squeeze tube and offered them around. The poke "salit" was rich and slightly bitter but good, and it provided us with the fresh greens that our standard menus of noodles, rice, and lentils lacked.

Into southern Virginia, the blossoms yielded to fruit on flowering trees. As we descended through a grassy meadow into Newport, I felt something crawling along my calf, and, when I glanced down, I spotted a legion of wood ticks creeping up my socks. After brushing them off, I spied hundreds of red berries nestled beneath green variegated leaves. Wild strawberries! Soon, Jeff, a blond hiker from Kansas, and Mark, a long-haired eighteen-year-old thru-hiker from Maryland, joined me, and together we filled a gallon-sized Ziploc bag before continuing into town. We made our first stop the general store, and soon each of us sat under the store's awning savoring dollops of vanilla ice cream smothered in fresh berries.

Through Virginia, the trail frequently followed abandoned wagon and carriage roads past remains of eighteenth- and nineteenth-century settlements. We often walked along rusted barbed-wire fences past decaying homesteads. One day, we encountered a fresh-water spring near where the hand-hewn timbers of a cabin had rotted away from an erect, fieldstone chimney. As we sat in the shade envying the former inhabitants their idyllic setting and simple life, I looked up and noticed that we were surrounded by cherry trees, their branches hanging heavy with ripe, red fruit. We soon emptied our quart water bottles and filled them with sweet cherries. We sat for an hour munching fruit and spewing pits into the brush. But, the cherries, too, posed uncomfortable side-effects, and, for the next several days, toilet paper was at a premium.

Further north, we plucked blackberries and raspberries from tangled thickets of briars. But, even fresh native fruits and berries could not mitigate the less desirable effects of summer—oppressive heat, humidity, and biting insects. The summer months, which ushered us through the trail's central states—Maryland, Pennsylvania, New Jersey, and New York—posed the most difficult miles of the trail for most of us. Not because of the difficulty of the terrain. On the contrary, passage through the central states brought with it a pestering boredom. The elevation of the mountains dipped below three thousand feet, there were few stunning vistas, and miles of trail coursed along roads and through congested urban areas. So frequent were the road crossings and encounters with developed areas that we had little sense of being in the woods at all. In the 161 miles through New Jersey and New York, the trail is crossed by 64 roads, an average of one in every two-and-a-half miles. The most auspicious road crossing is the Interstate 80 overpass, where the trail crosses the busy four-lane freeway *via* a fenced-in cement walkway. A green highway sign posted on the walkway alerts motorists that they're passing under the Appalachian Trail. In my travels between Washington, D.C. (where I lived the year prior to my hike), and my parents' home in Cincinnati, I passed under the bridge a half-dozen times, and, with each pass, I wondered how a hiker would feel to exit the woods onto a platform above four lanes of thundering semis and speeding automobiles.

During the summer, we constantly sought relief from the heat and boredom by wallowing in mountain streams and lakes. Evenings, we wrestled with the decision to bake in our sleeping bags and thus avoid the swarms of mosquitoes and gnats or to sleep—cooler—on top and awake to find our arms, legs, and faces swollen and itching from insect bites. I carried a bottle of jungle juice, a potent insect repellent developed for use by U.S. troops in Vietnam, which kept the bugs away but at a cost. It burned, and we joked, only half in jest, that it removed the top layer of skin. A few of us carried black-fly hoods—head-coverings sewn from mosquito netting—and evenings we resembled a corps of mournful beekeepers. Jimmy, a young man who hiked with us for several days and who had a knack for spinning macabre trail tales, used the hood as a theme for a fireside story about the Black-Fly Hood Murderer, who allegedly prowled the New Jersey woods, stalking unwary hikers and arriving in their camps after dark to hack them to bits with his hatchet.

Through the summer, our clothes stayed drenched in sweat, and our fluid intake escalated as the water levels of backcountry streams and springs dwindled. Gone were the cold, free-flowing springs of the South, the water of which we quaffed without a thought as to its purity; we were forced to take water from stagnant bogs and slow-moving creeks. We expended precious stove fuel boiling the water, or we doctored it with iodine tablets that left behind a rancid chemical taste. This routine also tended to turn our dinners an unappetizing shade of blue when the iodine reacted with the starch in our pasta. Increasingly, we left the trail to ask for tap water at nearby houses.

On the day we crossed Bear Mountain Bridge, which spans the Hudson River in New York, the temperature soared into the hundreds. As we climbed into shallow caves along the route, we spent blissful rest breaks in their constant, fifty-degree temperatures.

Through the midsummer months, we longed for the arrival of

fall and a return to the larger mountains we knew we would find in New England. It turned out that we encountered both on the same day. We had just exited New York and were covering the forty miles of trail through Connecticut. On August 6, as we began our hike, the heat, as usual, bore down on us, but, as the day progressed, a stiff wind blew in from the west and slowly began to sap the humidity from the air. When we ascended to the summit of Bear Mountain, a 2,316-foot peak near the Massachusetts border topped with a crumbling stone edifice built in 1885, the summer, with all its attendant misery, was gone. Crisp blue skies replaced the haze; billowy tufts of cumulus clouds floated by on the wind; and the air temperature plunged into the seventies, holding the promise of fall.

In Connecticut, we reentered the wilderness and began to scale larger mountains, mountains with views. The springs and streams, which had dwindled to murky, mosquito-infested puddles, again gave forth clean, cold water. When we descended Bear Mountain, crossed into Massachusetts, and descended into Sages Ravine, with its series of falls and deep pools, the air was too cool for swimming.

Once we arrived in New England, the trail still held a vestige of the wild fruit we had enjoyed in the South. On the day I crossed the open rock ledges leading to Bear Mountain, I suddenly noticed I had lost my companion, Paul Dillon, a long-legged strider, who normally blazed by me. A New Englander, Paul had recognized the scrub blueberry bushes, while I, absorbed in the views, had passed them by. He had slowed his pace, raking the bushes for fruit. Hours later, when he finally arrived in camp, his purple grin and red-stained fingers brought laughter from the rest of us, who had wondered what was taking him so long. For days afterward, the berries became a morning staple, finding their way into our pancakes, granola, and hot oatmeal.

By the time we crossed into New Hampshire on August 22, we had had our cold-weather woolens sent back to us. Crisp mornings found us layered in sweaters and windbreakers, and our evening fires provided warmth and smoke screens to drive away biting insects.

Then, in Maine, a state rich with birches, sugar maples, and oaks, the fall colors arrived on the heels of Hurricane David, which blasted the northern woods with wind and cold rain in early September. By the time we reached Monson, the last major town for the trail's final 116 miles, the frost had tinged the maples blaze-red, the birches mottled entire hillsides in gold, and the oaks dappled the mountains in bursts of orange and yellow.

Our ascent of Mount Katahdin brought with it a taste of winter. Ice layered Thoreau Spring, situated a mile below the summit, and the wind pierced our layers of nylon and wool. But, if it was a day of ice, it was also a day of fire. Sprawling away from the base of the mountain, fall's flaming colors fringed the cool, blue ponds of the Lake Country.

Over the course of five months, we had traced the cycle of the seasons, from the wintry peaks of the southern Appalachians in April, through the months of spring and summer, to the fall and the brink of another winter in central Maine. Though I have lost the intimacy with the seasons since my hike, I retain the sense of perfect order, of graceful succession and surrender, and of the bold brilliance of fall leaves as they yield to death.

CHAPTER FOUR

Our Gang

I proceed for all who are or have been young men, To tell the secret of my nights and days, To celebrate the need of comrades.

WALT WHITMAN
"IN PATHS UNTRODDEN"

 Y THE TIME DAN AND I ENTERED VIRGINIA JUNE 1, we had become a trio. Nick Gelesko, known on the trail as the Michigan Granddad, a fifty-seven-year-old retired engineer from Dawagiac, Michigan, had joined us. By the time we reached New Jersey, we were a foursome, having adopted Paul Dillon, a twenty-year-old former competitive skier from Peterboro, New Hampshire. From then on, we were virtually inseparable.

Of all the trail's gifts, none was more precious to me than that of friendship. We were a corps of men and women united by our common love of nature, by our shared needs and experiences, and our affection for one another was as real and enduring as the love of brothers and sisters. We lived side by side, and we shared of ourselves—our thoughts, our fears, our hopes, our experiences past and present—as freely as we shared our food and shelter.

I remember nights in the company of trail friends, some spent around campfires, others in open, star-lit fields, some under rain-pummeled tin roofs, many beside churning brooks, and I remember talking, sometimes for hours, about love, death, God, spirit, nature. Or about more mundane concerns: blisters, bent tent poles, wet boots. Perhaps more significant than the ease with which we discussed our feelings were the remarkably unselfconscious stretches of silence when we were content just to have close friends nearby.

Evenings, each of us followed his own interests. At dusk, Dan often retired with his penny whistle to a stream, where his notes mingled with the melodic tumble of water. Paul, our trailside Lord Byron, frequently scribbled odes about love or nature in his journal, which he shared with us around evening fires. Each night after dinner, Nick, squatting on his haunches, meticulously measured, mixed, and stirred his beloved chocolate pudding, as his baritone voice hummed some forgotten ballad from the 1950s. The rest of us always knew that, when he finished, we would find a dollop of dessert left in his cook pot for each of us. While my colleagues pursued their evening diversions, I pursued my own, reclining against a tree and recording the whole wonderful scene in my journal.

These are the things I remember about my trail family.

Dan

 AN, A FORMER ARCHITECTURAL PLANNER FOR A MAJOR oil corporation, had left a promising fast-track career to walk in the woods. He may have left the job, but he retained his gift for organizing, leading, orchestrating, planning. Dan was our field marshal, who, perhaps more than the rest of us, kept his eye on our daily progress, constantly measuring the months against the miles and making sure we reached Katahdin before winter snows closed the mountain down in October. In spite of his drive to cover the miles, he was just as attuned to natural wonders as the rest of us—perhaps even more so—and he frequently called our attention to plants, animals, or birds that had escaped our notice.

Unlike Dan, I had become oblivious to accumulated mileage and more inclined to amble and roost when I found a snug nest along the way. Had it not been for Dan and his intense desire to drive north, I suspect I might have whiled away the summer, lazing in mountain lakes or stooped over fresh-scented flowers, and might have missed my date with Katahdin altogether. On most occasions, we yielded to Dan's scheduling and advanced at his pace, but not always happily.

In mid-Pennsylvania, after Nick had slowed his pace to hike with his wife, Gwen, who had joined us for a couple of weeks, and before Paul had joined our group, Dan and I were again a twosome. We decided to do an easy day out of Duncannon to a campsite sixteen miles away. Once we were out of town and over the broad bridge spanning the Susquehanna River, Dan blasted ahead, while I throttled back, taking extended rest stops and rummaging through my food bag for the candy and other sweet treats that always attended my departure from town. At 5:30 p.m., I arrived at our scheduled stop, ready to relax. Instead of finding Dan scribing in his journal, I discovered a hand-written note. He had arrived in camp early, become restless, and decided to push on an additional eleven miles, making for a twenty-seven-mile day.

Hiking, like most other endurance activities, is a mental as well as physical pursuit. That is particularly true when you face high-mileage days. Even hikers in prime condition suffer aches, pains, and fatigue after long miles. Most often, when we confronted twenty-plus-mile days, they were planned, allowing us time to psych ourselves up for the long stretches. In the days prior to a long-mile hump, we ate more, rested more. Consider that a hiker who maintains a three-mile-an-hour pace, which is about as fast as one can travel mountainous terrain on foot with a loaded pack, will walk continuously for a full nine hours to cover twenty-seven miles. That includes no time for eating, drinking, resting, or smelling the flowers. Discovering at 5:30 p.m. that I faced an additional eleven miles did not make me a happy camper.

I would have stayed the night where I was, but there were a few complicating factors: Dan carried the guidebook, half of the tent, and half the stove. Without a guidebook, I had no means for gauging my progress over the remaining eleven miles other than by multiplying my average speed (three miles per hour) by the elapsed time and stopping when my watch indicated that I had covered the distance. I also was left without means for protecting myself from the elements, and I was not about to hack down perfectly healthy trees to make a den. At the time, I saw one option: to bust ass and catch Dan.

If I hustled, allowing no food or water breaks, I surmised I would reach the shelter by about 9:10 p.m., a half-hour past dusk. That is, provided I could find the blue-blazed side trail to the shelter in the darkness. Never mind the hundreds of fist-sized rocks—Pennsylvania is famous for them—that tottered with each step and gouged the soles, and never mind the thriving population of rattlesnakes inhabiting the area—Pennsylvania's second most notable distinction. I wolfed down two high-energy breakfast bars, gulped down a liter of water, and set out.

At about 7:00 p.m., still seven-and-a-half-miles from my destination, I passed a group of day-hikers on the trail. Had they seen Dan, the low-life who had abandoned me a few miles back? Yes, a high-school-aged girl answered.

"He figured you might be a little upset," she said.

"And be careful up ahead," she called after me. "There was a big rattlesnake coiled in the middle of the trail!"

I never saw the rattlesnake, but then I didn't look for it. Anger, it seemed, has a wonderful way of dampening one's fear.

By 9:15 and now moving through dusk, I slowed, looking for the blue-blazed trail to the shelter. Blue blazes are difficult enough to spot in the daylight, let alone after dark. Besides, during July, such side trails are frequently overgrown and barely discernible. By 9:20, now following the beam of my miniflashlight and with my thighs twitching and the soles of my feet feeling as if I had trodden across hot glass shards, I still hadn't spotted the blaze. As I was about to roll out my bag in the weeds and eat a cold dinner, I finally spied it. Soon, I was wheeling along toward the shelter. When I reached it, Dan greeted me tentatively. Until my temper calmed, I said nothing at all.

What followed had all the makings of a backwoods lovers' spat. I explained that I could appreciate his yen to cover more miles but didn't appreciate being left with no stove, shelter, or guidebook. Dan sympathized but went on to explain that this was his trip and that he was going to do it his way. That hurt. It reawakened the feelings I had confronted in Georgia, the fear that I couldn't keep pace with him, that I was bogging him down.

I suggested that perhaps it would be best if we split up, dividing the gear, he taking the stove and I taking the shelter and both of us making arrangements to acquire the additional equipment we needed. I'm thankful that it didn't come to that. We both seemed to realize that, after investing so much time and energy in the relationship, it would have been a shame to dissolve it. I know I would have missed his company, and I suspect he would have missed mine. Besides, what would our backcountry neighbors have said when they learned that Dan and Dave, one of the more stable trail marriages, had separated? The next morning, we continued north, our union intact after surviving our first quarrel.

The next time Dan's drive for miles provoked a rift, we were four—Nick and Paul had joined us—and this time our voting bloc prevailed. It happened in Vermont on August 12, the day we hiked through the spruce-clad northern Berkshires to the 3,491-foot summit of Mount Greylock, the highest peak in Massachusetts. That day, we confronted some of the worst weather the Appalachians can muster: The temperature hovered just above freezing. Wind and cold rain stung our faces and hands, and we frequently stepped ankle-deep into mucky spruce bogs as we picked our way to the top. By early afternoon, we arrived at Bascom Lodge, an ample, rough-hewn summit house built in 1937. Once over the threshold, I was convinced we had perished on the trail and had passed into hiker heaven. A fire blazed in each of two three-foot-square fireplaces, one in each of the two thirty-by-twenty-five-foot great rooms. There was hot coffee, hamburgers, junk food. Old furniture—great comfortable couches and easy chairs—sat in the warmth of the fires.

After peeling off our wet clothes, we sat by the fire sipping hot coffee. When Dan suggested that we take it easy for an hour or so, then push back out into the rain for a few more miles, we were incredulous. We held fast and finally reached a compromise: We would stay the night at the lodge and make up the lost mileage over the next few days. The four of us helped wax the scarred wooden floors in exchange for the night's lodging. I spent most of the evening perched at a wooden table, facing a bank of large picture windows. Through the glass, I glimpsed the wind-buffeted spruce trees and the swirling fog and rain—the very misery we had escaped—and I slept that night thoroughly content with our decision to stay. I suspect Dan did, too.

AYBE DAN WAS DRIVEN, BUT HE WAS ALSO ENDOWED with other attributes that allow people to thrive in the wilderness. Though slight in stature, at five feet, ten inches tall and 145 pounds, and with straight, sandy-blond hair and brown eyes, Dan was rock-steady courageous and tough. Over the five months we spent together, I never saw his courage falter. He was crazy, too. Crazy to expand his margins and experience new things. More than once, in the midst of a cold spring rain, I watched him strip off his clothes and step under a frigid waterfall or plunge into an icy pool just to savor the rush it would bring.

He demonstrated those hard-edged qualities again and again over our months together, but never more convincingly than on the trail that led us out of Hanover, New Hampshire, in late August.

We had just left the road and had begun our ascent back into the mountains. I led and soon pulled away from my three companions. About a half-mile up the trail, I encountered a hand-written note attached to some evergreen boughs that had been arranged across the trail. The note warned of a bees' nest ahead and advised us to skirt around it. I looked ahead and saw a hole two feet in diameter seething with yellow jackets, and I called back to the others a couple hundred yards behind to be careful. Nick, ahead of Dan and Paul, nodded, though in retrospect it is clear he hadn't understood my warning. I veered into the brush, passed around the nest, and continued up the trail.

In seconds, I heard Nick shout, and I turned just in time to see him break into a run. He had overlooked the sign and had continued right over the nest. Though he had escaped being stung, he had pitched the bees into a protective frenzy. Then, I watched and listened—helplessly—as Dan began flailing and emitting a horrible series of screams, each marking a sting. I wanted to run and help him, but I realized that there was nothing any of us could do; we would just have become targets ourselves. The attack—and the screaming—lasted for nearly a minute before Dan reached a safe distance from the nest, and the swarm retreated. Once it was over, I reeled from spent adrenaline. All of us did.

Anyone who has ever been the victim of a yellow jacket knows the instant, throbbing acid burn of a single sting. In all, Dan had suffered twenty-six stings. The bees had pierced his bare face, arms, and legs and had swarmed inside his shorts and shirt. He was a mass of red, acid-oozing welts, and I realized that if he were allergic to the venom, as many people are, he would die quickly. His breathing tube would swell shut, and he would asphyxiate.

Within minutes, Dan had completely regained his calm. He sat quietly on a rock, focusing, pulling himself back together, as Nick, Paul, and I buzzed frantically around him offering to help, though I'm not sure how we could have eased his discomfort. He declined our offers and continued to sit. Within five minutes of the attack, he rose and, unbelievably, started walking back toward the hive.

"I dropped my walking stick," he said.

Dan had found the stick, a twisted, gnarly branch, on Springer Mountain, and he had grown attached to it. I would learn later that he aimed to deposit it, in a private ceremony on Mount Katahdin, making it a 2,100-mile stick. He crept cautiously to within three feet of the hive, picked up his staff, returned to where we stood, climbed into his pack, and continued up the trail. Meanwhile, the rest of us—stunned—fumbled into our pack straps and followed.

Some days later, I, too, became a yellow-jacket casualty. Though stung only four times, I cursed and shrieked, wheeled and spun, flailing at unseen adversaries. Afterward, as I stood panting and shaking, I wanted to sit in self-pity and lick my wounds, but, remembering Dan's example, I glanced ahead to the next white blaze and kept on walking.

Nick

E MET NICK GELESKO OVER A VEGETARIAN DINNER at the Inn in Hot Springs, North Carolina. The inn, a restored nineteenth-century resort hotel, had once served an upscale clientele that sought the healing powers of the hot mineral springs located a few blocks away. Though the springs had passed from vogue years earlier, by 1979, the inn—which featured bountiful vegetarian meals, New Age music, and hundreds of books—reigned as a mecca for hungry hikers.

Seated at the round wooden table, Nick wore a khaki shirt bearing an Appalachian Trail patch and a matching pair of khaki pants. He was Sean Connery handsome, with a tanned face, sharp features, bright brown eyes, and, like Connery, a bald pate. Dressed as he was in his khaki uniform and surrounded by an air of confidence and authority, I initially mistook him for a park ranger. Through the meal, Nick assumed the role of table host, drawing out some of the more reluctant hikers and sharing bits of his own stories. I soon detected in him irrepressible charm and charisma.

Over the ensuing summer, those attributes made Nick an endearing sidekick. They also became a secret weapon, one we employed countless times in asking for—and receiving—favored treatment from townsfolk along the way.

Because of his age, Nick, at first, posed a fatherly threat to some of us younger men who were out on the trail to exert our indepen-

dence, to find our own way and shed the tethers of adult authority. He had fought in the South Pacific during World War II (our
fathers' war), he had raised his children to adulthood, and his attitudes were decidedly conservative. At many of our fireside chats
early on, he represented the establishment point of view while we
argued in behalf of the new order.

But the trail, along with the social healing brought on by the
1970s, had softened many of Nick's attitudes about the younger
generation, just as it had altered our attitudes regarding his. One
night, near the end of the trail, Nick discussed his relationship
with his son, who had opted for Canada during the Vietnam War
rather than face the draft. As a veteran, Nick had initially responded by severing ties with his son and his family, but, eventually, his love for his son and his increasing sympathy for the young
men who had become entangled in the complexities of the conflict
changed his thinking, and he and his wife, Gwen, had made a trip
to Canada.

As our relationship developed and we became more closely
bound by our shared experiences, Nick and the rest of us found
common ground on many issues. Soon our age differences were as
insignificant as the regions of the country we hailed from.

Nick ultimately became one of my closest friends and companions, a man whom I still admire as much as anyone I've ever known.
Whatever courage it took for me—a twenty-three-year-old
man—to face the wild, his was greater. Though the body of a fifty-
seven-year-old man can't cover the miles at the same clip as men
less than half his age, he kept pace with us, never complaining
about his ailing knees and feet, while many of the rest of us
vented our physical woes almost nightly.

As for our secret weapon: Nick was charming, so charming, in
fact, that I'm convinced that, given time, he might have persuaded Donald Trump to turn over his casinos, all of his rental
properties, all his worldly possessions, and all of his lands, and that,
once the deal was struck, somehow Nick would have left Trump
feeling that he—not Nick—had profited in the transaction. What's
more, Nick was confident enough to ask for anything from anybody,

and his older, more mature countenance stood him in good stead with local folks, many of whom were distrustful of us younger guys. The combined effect of his charm, chutzpah, and maturity became our ticket to a bounty of special privileges.

The first time I saw Nick work his magic, I ascribed it to luck. Dan and I had arrived at the road crossing where a little-traveled Virginia highway cut the trail, and we had arranged to meet Nick, who was some distance behind, in town. While Dan and I baked in the sun, our thumbs eagerly thrust in the air, car after car inhabited by sour-faced people zoomed by. Some of the drivers were so leery of us that they swerved into the oncoming traffic lane to be sure we didn't leap through the open windows and commandeer their vehicles. After we had spent nearly an hour of smiling, waving, and looking as harmless as possible, a huge Buick slowed, swung onto the berm, and stopped. I immediately recognized Nick's tan porkpie hat and grinning face through the windshield of the passenger seat.

"You fellas need a lift?" he asked.

After we loaded our packs into the trunk, Nick introduced us to the driver, a middle-aged man whom he addressed with the familiarity of an old friend. Thoroughly charmed, the man had agreed to drive us into town, to wait while we bought our groceries and washed our clothes at the local laundromat, and then to shuttle us back to the trailhead to resume our hike.

The next time it happened, I began to suspect that there was more to Nick's good fortune than simple dumb luck. On a similarly isolated stretch of highway a few days farther north, we repeated the same scenario, with Dan and me—thumbs in the air—ruefully watching an armada of cars and trucks roll past. Then, a battered flatbed swung off the road and stopped, and a familiar, grinning face topped with a porkpie hat poked from the passenger's window.

"Come on over," Nick called through the window. "I'd like for you guys to meet my friend, Martin, who's been kind enough to give us a lift into town."

From then on, in a slightly skewed version of the old hitchhiker's ruse in which the alluring blonde flags down a lift while her male friend hides in the bushes, Nick acted as our front man. He stood prominently on the highway, while Dan and I lingered just out of sight until Nick called us over to meet our chauffeur. Once we got to town, we loaded our packs at the local store, and Dan and I sat on the store stoop while our envoy roved through the store lot, scanning the parked cars for those that offered ample room for three hikers and their packs. Then, he waited. When the owners arrived, he launched into his routine, which went something like this:

"Good afternoon (morning, evening), ma'am (sir, young man, young lady), my name is Nick, and I'm out hiking the Appalachian Trail. I just want you to know that my buddies and I sure are enjoying the scenery around (town name here). In fact, it's some of the most beautiful country we've seen so far, and the people sure are friendly. Hey, by the way, we're trying to find a way back up (highway name and number here) to the trail junction so we can continue our hike. Would you know of anyone around here who might be willing, say, to earn a few extra bucks by giving us a lift?"

More often than not, the first contact would assent, but, if not the first, always the second. Soon, Nick would motion us over to meet his new friend. Often, *en route*, the drivers handed us a couple of cold beers, a bag of chicken legs, or a ham sandwich, and, in spite of Nick's offer to pay for the lift, few of them accepted our money. They were just happy to help us out.

After weeks of practice, Nick became thoroughly proficient at procuring food, drink, and transportation from strangers, yet we exhausted our vocabularies in searching for a word to describe what he did. It really wasn't "scamming." Sure, Nick sometimes exaggerated the direness of our circumstances by insisting that we were "bone weary" or by claiming that our hunger or misery was so abject that we might perish if we didn't get to town soon. But, he never knowingly deceived anyone, and he never attempted to force anyone to help us. In some ways, I think the donors benefited from their contact with us, particularly the drivers, who often seemed hungry for company and welcomed our companionship. And, everyone enjoyed our trail stories. But still, what to call Nick's magical process? Finally, after weeks of searching, we fixed on a term for Nick's natural aptitude: "Geleskoing," derived from his last name.

Gelesko-ing: the use of tact and persuasion by Appalachian Trail hikers to influence local townsfolk to provide goods and services free of charge.

We applied the word in the following ways:

"Where did you get that sandwich?"

"I *Geleskoed* it from some picnickers a few miles back on the trail."

"How did you get into town?"

"I *Geleskoed* a ride from a nice couple returning from church."

"Where did you stay last night?"

"I *Geleskoed* a family into letting me stay in their guest bedroom."

Among Nick's most notable coups, I count the following: We were staying the night in a ski lodge on Sugarloaf Mountain in central Maine. The lodge, a circular structure with a massive central fireplace and walls of windows looking out on the surrounding peaks, was abandoned but had been left open as a refuge to hikers. We laid our bags out on the wooden benches surrounding the fireplace and stoked the flames from the ample pile of firewood provided by the caretaker.

Midafternoon, I heard a clang, then the clattering of gears, and ran to one of the windows. I turned to the lift cables, which had sat idle since we had arrived in the early afternoon, just in time to see Nick's hat through the rear window of a gondola descending toward the mountain's base. Where was he going? He had left without giving us a clue. It turned out that the caretaker, who just happened to be in the lodge, had been Geleskoed into operating the lift in spite of dangerous winds. Before we could probe him for information regarding Nick's mission, he had left the lodge and begun hiking down the mountain.

Several hours passed, and the winds increased. At one point, the wind howled so fiercely that, when I stepped outside to dump a pot of dishwater, the wind ripped the pot from my hand and threw the water back in my face with such force that it stung.

More time passed. Still no sign of Nick. Just before dusk, I heard the gears grind into motion, and, far down the mountain, I could see a red gondola ascending the cable. The car bucked and swayed like a carnival ride run amok, and, when it neared each of the towers that supported the lines, it stopped. Inside, I could see Nick, swinging back and forth, captive in the round red pendulum. He would swing left, toward the tower, then as he swung right, away from the obstacle, the motor would again engage, and the car would advance, each time barely missing the tower on its back-swing. The process was repeated at each of the half-dozen towers, and the lift operator at the base of the mountain would gauge the rhythm of the swinging car as he rocked it past the tower. At last, the car entered the gondola shed, the engine stopped, and Nick emerged carrying two grocery bags.

One of the bags contained three half-gallons of ice cream. The other contained several bags of cookies and a bottle of wine. It turned out that Nick had made his tempest-tossed voyage in search of sweets, and, as we all attacked the bounty of confections, he explained his adventure.

Struck by an irrepressible craving for sugar, Nick had consulted his map. Noting that the road at the base of the mountain led into Stratton, he had approached the caretaker (who also served as the lift operator) for a ride to the bottom. When the caretaker refused, explaining that the wind conditions made it unsafe to operate the lift, Nick persisted. Finally, the caretaker agreed to send Nick down the mountain. Once at the base, Nick had persuaded—Geleskoed, rather—some kindly local folks into giving him a lift to the grocery store. After cleaning out the ice-cream freezer at the store, he had persuaded another kindly local to give him a lift back to the gon-dola. Then, after waiting futilely for a full hour for the winds to calm, he had cajoled the lift operator, who by now had returned to the base, into giving him a ride back to the top. As a result of his expedition, Nick may well rank as the only Appalachian Trail hiker ever to risk death for a few half-gallons of Breyer's vanilla ice cream.

Then there was the night in Rangeley, Maine.

We arrived in Rangeley on September 6, driven from the woods by the tail end of Hurricane David, which whipped the surface of Lake Rangeley into a froth of rolling white caps. Rangeley is a quiet New England resort town, set on the shores of the lake and crowded with quaint shops and restaurants competing for the tourist trade.

In several towns along the trail, local churches had opened their doors to hikers, providing them a place to sleep for the night. According to the scuttlebutt on the trail, a Protestant church in Rangeley was one such place. We had made our requisite stop at the local grocery store and, after scampering along rain-drenched streets, found our way to the church just after dark.

Once inside, we made ourselves at home in the recreation room, which featured a full kitchen and a number of banquet tables. We soon commenced the ritualistic food binge that accompanied our arrivals in town by preparing heaping root beer floats. Nick had wandered into the sanctuary and had found a Bible, and, as we sat slurping our floats, he began flipping through it, looking for familiar passages. Soon, we were engaged in a discussion of Christian ethics and the role of Christ as teacher and provider, which inspired us to give thanks for having such a snug refuge from the storm.

Though we frequently discussed religious philosophy, we didn't often discuss the specific tenets of Christianity. But, this night the topic was Christ: His resurrection, the redemption He offered the world's sinners. Christian love, we determined, whether the doctrine behind it was or was not the only way to salvation, was a beautiful force at work in the world. After all, we agreed, though the congregation of this church did not know us, they had opened their doors to us.

At 8:00 p.m., our discussion of Christian love was brought to an abrupt halt when the church caretaker arrived and, explaining that hikers were no longer welcome to stay in the church, threw us out into the bleak, cold night.

We made our way from the sanctuary into the gutter, arriving some minutes later at Doc Grant's, a local watering hole perhaps best known for its alleged location precisely halfway between the equator and the North Pole. The placemats at the bar depict a map bisected by a line. In the upper half is a sketch of an Eskimo clad in mukluks and a fur coat. In the lower half is a rendering of a hula girl in grass skirt.

We sidled up to the bar, ordered a round of cold beers, and watched reruns of the "Andy Griffith Show." Meanwhile, we had no notion of where we might be sleeping that night. The hotels in town were decidedly upscale and priced beyond our budgets, and the hurricane had made conditions outdoors insufferable. Our tents would have been ripped to tatters by the wind and rain. We had asked—begged really—a place to stay from every patron at the bar but received no firm offers. On our march from the church to the bar, we had noticed a theater marquee sheltered by a large overhang and decided that, if worse came to worst, we could always sleep there. For the first time on our trek, we were plum out of tricks. Or, so we thought. That's when Nick went to work.

While the rest of us sat at the bar, Nick got a few dollars' worth of quarters and a phone book and walked over to the pay phone. First, he called the local hotels. It was prime tourist season, and there were no available rooms. Then, he called all the local churches. Still no luck. After learning the names of the town's elected officials from the barkeep, he called the mayor. Even he balked. Then, Nick called the chief of police and finally struck pay dirt. Smiling, he rejoined us at the bar.

"Our ride will be here in five minutes," he said, returning to his beer. And, so it was. In a few minutes, the chief of police, clad in a rain slicker, entered the bar, asked for Nick, introduced himself, and ushered us out of the bar into a waiting cruiser. We soon arrived at the police station, our home for the night. It was the first and only night I've spent in jail, and I couldn't have been happier.

NLY ONCE DID I SEE GELESKO'S CHARM FAIL. WE HAD arrived at Farmers Mills Shelter, set two hundred feet off a back road near Stormville, New York. The shelter, our scheduled destination for the night, turned out to be a fetid, cinder-block hovel surrounded by heaps of trash and a mosquito-infested swamp. Gelesko took one look at it and decreed that he wasn't about to sleep there. Soon, he moved on up the country road to make other arrangements. With the rest of us in tow, he approached a nearby house, which boasted a large garage, and knocked at the door. When a middle-aged woman cracked open the door, he began his pitch.

"Good afternoon, ma'am. My name is Nick Gelesko, and a few buddies and I are hiking the Appalachian Trail."

"Yes?" she asked suspiciously.

"Well, it's been so darned hot the past few days, and that shelter up the road is really a mess, you know with trash and mosquitoes, and I was wondering if you know of anyone around here who might have, well, say, a garage where we might roll out our bags and sleep the night."

At that point, Nick, having emphasized the word garage, turned and casually glanced at its counterpart around the corner of the house.

"Sure don't," the woman answered without hesitating.

Undaunted, Nick continued. "You know a *garage* or some place we could lay out our bags? We sure would be grateful."

"No, I'm sorry."

"You know, if someone were to have a *garage*, we'd be more than happy to do a little cleaning up to help pay for the kindness."

The three of us stood within ear shot, and, frankly, we couldn't believe what we were hearing. Was it actually possible for someone—anyone—to resist being Geleskoed by Gelesko himself? Gradually, the woman began to soften.

"Well, I can't let you stay in my garage, because my husband's out of town, and he wouldn't approve. But, there's a young guy up the road who lives in a barn, and he might take you in."

On her advice, we pushed up the road until we arrived at a red barn that had been converted to a suitable, though drafty, residence. Nick knocked at the door, and a young man answered. In less than a minute, Nick waved us all toward the door. His magic was back. He introduced us to our host for the night, and soon we were upstairs, sipping cold beers and flipping through the man's record supply, blissed out on rock 'n' roll music.

Paul

 HEN WE ENCOUNTERED TWENTY-YEAR-OLD NEW HAMP-shire native Paul Dillon in Pennsylvania, he was making his third attempt on the Appalachian Trail. Paul had begun the trail at Springer Mountain in 1976, reaching as far north as the Cumberland Gap in Pennsylvania. He set out on the trail again in 1978 and reached as far as the Blue Ridge Parkway in Virginia. He returned to the trail in 1979, starting his hike where he had left off in Pennsylvania, and Dan and I met him just north of Port Clinton. As it turned out, the encounter would benefit all of us.

Dan and I had suffered our first major battle of wills a few days earlier over the planned sixteen-mile day that evolved into a twenty-seven-mile marathon, and, though we were speaking to one another, our relationship lacked any semblance of brotherly affection. Paul's inclusion in the group immediately eased the tension between us. At the same time, we offered Paul the two things he seemed to need most. First was companionship. He had mistimed his first and second ventures on the trail and had missed the mass of northbound thru-hikers. After spending days and nights alone, he had decided to leave the trail. The second thing we offered Paul was Dan's knack for organization and goal setting, which would impose a schedule on Paul and the rest of us and would guarantee to lead us to the summit of Katahdin by summer's end.

Despite his thwarted attempts on the trail, Paul possessed an

AS FAR AS THE EYE CAN SEE

aptitude for wilderness travel. While Dan and Nick tended at times to muscle their way along, confronting obstacles with will and determination, Paul seemed inclined to abide by whatever nature threw his way and to try to make the best of it. As far as Paul was concerned, whatever we encountered along the trail was okay as long as he was able to glean some significance from it. For Paul, miles did not measure linear distance so much as they traced units of experience. Paul sought the sadness, the happiness, the beauty, the wisdom lurking in the wilderness, and he translated those things into the verses and songs he composed along the way. While the rest of us orally recounted the highlights of our days as we sat around campfires, Paul was often inclined to apply his thoughts to paper and, once finished, to share them with the group.

Paul had carried his penchant for poetry so far as to have had a friend embroider a verse onto the front flap of his green nylon framepack. The verse, taken from *On the Loose*, Jerry and Renny Russell's book on adventure and the environment, reads:

> So why do we do it?
> What good is it?
> Does it teach you anything?
> Like determination?
> Invention?
> Improvisation?
> Foresight?
> Hindsight?
> Love?
> Art?
> Music?
> Religion?
> Strength or patience or accuracy or quickness or
>   tolerance or which wood will burn and how
>   long is a day and how far is a mile and how
>   delicious is water and smoky green-pea soup?
> And how to rely on yourself?

The verse embraced the essence of the trail quest, but, more than that, it captured the grace and rhythm that seemed to govern everything Paul did, whether writing a poem or traversing a ridge.

I will forever picture Paul ambling along the trail, smiling and shirtless, his lanky six-foot-one-inch frame clad only in blue corduroy Ocean Pacific shorts, knee-high gaiters, socks, and boots, and with his shoulder-length brown hair bound by a red bandanna tied pirate-style.

A former competitive downhill skier and college tennis player, Paul had been an accomplished athlete long before taking up the trail. Though he was lean, his strength and endurance powered him past most other thru-hikers on long ascents, and his physical poise and skier's balance allowed him to dance effortlessly down steep, rock-strewn descents where most hikers crept cautiously along.

I didn't fully appreciate just how graceful Paul was on his feet until we reached the White Mountains in New Hampshire, where the open, treeless ridges allowed us to glimpse other hikers from miles away. On the afternoon that Dan and I arrived at Lakes of the Clouds Hut, nestled below the summit of Mount Washington, we dumped our packs and climbed to the top of Mount Monroe, a secondary peak a few hundred yards from the hut.

From our perch a couple of hundred feet above the trail, we watched hikers wend their way along the rocky path heading north. As practitioners of the art of walking, we had developed a habit of evaluating the style of other foot travelers. Among those we scrutinized that day, some cullumphed along like human jackhammers, assaulting the trail with their heavy footfalls. Others surged ahead like jack rabbits, stopping to rest at two-hundred-yard intervals before surging ahead again. A few labored painfully along like arthritic octogenarians, pausing after each step to peer ahead, hoping to glimpse the hut and the termination of their misery. After watching them pass, Dan and I fixed on a lone hiker who, unlike the others, eased effortlessly across the open ridge.

"Look at that guy move," Dan said, pointing.

"God, he's graceful," I said. And, he was. Every step, every aspect of his stride, from the bend of his knees to the pivot of his torso to the plant of his walking stick, was as fluid as a brook coursing its way between and over the boulders of a streambed.

It wasn't until he neared the base of the mountain that we recognized the familiar green backpack and red bandanna as belonging to our own poet laureate, Paul.

CHAPTER FIVE

Linear Community

Whatever concerns I had about this trail lacking human companionship were resolved this evening. There are nineteen hikers and two dogs wedged into the shelter. Further cramping our space are hikers' packs and foodbags, which hang like ripe fruit from the rafters—to keep them from the mice, rats, and skunks who also call this place home. There are hikers here from Indiana, Illinois, Ohio, Tennessee, North Carolina, Massachusetts, Virginia, and Georgia, and, though we all have different backgrounds and come from different parts of the country, we are unified by our shared love for the wilderness. Here are nineteen strangers existing so peaceably, sharing food, thoughts, equipment, and trail tips under conditions that would pitch most city dwellers into panic. What is it about our society that inhibits such wonderful—and spontaneous—acceptance and sense of community?

MAY 6, 1979
RUSSELL FIELD SHELTER
GREAT SMOKY MOUNTAINS NATIONAL PARK

ANY PEOPLE ENVISION THE APPALACHIAN TRAIL AS a remote, isolated wilderness path where hikers pass days—even weeks—in utter solitude and with no access to roads or towns for supplies and companionship.

Even some novice trail hikers maintain such a skewed vision of the trail. A pair of would-be thru-hikers I met near Springer Mountain in 1987, for instance, believed that, once a person had set out on the trail, there was no means of egress and that the hiker was committed to traveling at least as far as Harpers Ferry, nearly one thousand miles north, before he could bail out or acquire fresh supplies. As a result, the two wretched souls carried nearly one hundred pounds of gear each, including extra boots and a two-month supply of food.

I'll acknowledge that the image of a hiker confronting the eastern wilds alone is romantic. Perhaps the trail's pioneers, including Earl Shaffer, who logged the first end-to-end hike in 1948, did experience such isolation. By 1979, the trail attracted dozens of hopeful thru-hikers and thousands of "weekenders" or "short-timers" who visited the trail for one- or two-day hikes. According to Appalachian Trail Conference statistics, as many as four million people visit the trail each year.

No, the Appalachian Trail is not a lonely place. On the contrary, Dan and I passed few days without encountering at least one other person on the trail. In the more popular sections—through national parks—we often met and talked with dozens of people. For those who sought isolation, the trail's human population may have been a disappointment, but for others—most hikers, really—the thriving backcountry society only enhanced the experience. Any hiker who has spent weeks along the route knows that the real story of the Appalachian Trail is found among the people who walk it.

The social quality of the trail inspired Nancy Sills, wife of Normal Sills, a Connecticut native who thru-hiked the trail in 1985, to dub the trail a "linear community," and, of all the descriptions applied to the trail, I find hers most fitting. My experience is that, if the trail were a community, it was a community predicated on trust, fellowship, and sharing—values that too often seem lacking in the more "civilized" society we had left behind.

During our days of hiking through the Smokies—then the most visited national park in the country—we met dozens of other hikers. Many, like us, were thru-hikers bound for Maine, but there were also many day-hikers and weekend backpackers. I recall the night we slept in Russell Field Shelter, tucked in a hardwood grove seventeen miles south of Clingmans Dome, the highest point on the trail. As daylight waned, hikers continued to arrive at the shelter until nineteen people and two dogs occupied a space designed to accommodate twelve. Among them was a woman who lived in a teepee in Massachusetts; another woman and her bearded boyfriend, both from North Carolina, who had packed in a glass bottle of tequila; two college students from Dayton, Ohio; and others who hailed from Indiana, Georgia, Virginia, and Illinois.

Because of the cramped conditions, late-comers and the two dogs slept on the floor. Once all of us and our gear were ensconced inside, the nineteen packs and accompanying foodbags—of orange, blue, red, maroon, turquoise, and brown nylon—hung like ripe fruit from the shelter's rafters.

That night, chatter filled the shelter as hikers swapped backpacking tips, compared equipment, and talked of faraway home towns. For me, it marked the first time I had experienced the communion shared among hikers in the backcountry. It did not matter who you were, where you were from, or how much you were worth. If you were a backpacker, you were okay.

The rigors of life on the trail tended to screen out most undesirables, while those same rigors tended to unify those of us who were tough and committed enough to forge on. We climbed the same mountains; we plodded through the same rainstorms; we suffered the same aches and pains as our bodies adapted to the physical challenge of fifteen- to twenty-mile days. We drank from the same springs; we stopped at the same towns to resupply; we experienced the same insatiable hunger—which I termed "hiker's disease"—as our bodies metabolized as many as six thousand calories a day. We carried the same equipment; we swatted the same mosquitoes; we slept in the same three-sided, rough-hewn shelters. And, we shared the same quest.

We learned to depend on one another. If a hiker failed to arrive in camp by nightfall, we mounted a search party and set out with our flashlights. The night we camped at Ice Water Springs, four miles north of Newfound Gap, the midway point of the Smokies, a hiker in the shelter expressed concern that his companion had not yet arrived in camp a half-hour after dark. Though beautiful by day, the Smokies posed certain hazards by night, among them bears and the roving herds of three-hundred-pound wild boars that use their formidable tusks to scavenge for food after dark. We organized a search party, left the security of the fence-enclosed shelter, and followed our flashlight beams into the darkness. As I pushed up the trail past the darkened groves of hardwoods, a line from Robert Frost's poem "Stopping by Woods" kept tumbling through my mind: "The woods are lovely, dark and deep. . . ." And, they were. Every sound and shadow teased my imagination. Rocks wore faces, tree trunks sheltered gnomes, branches shivered and squeaked.

Within a half mile, I detected a beam of light sweeping the trail ahead and realized that we had found our lost hiker. He had taken a wrong turn at a trail junction a few tenths of a mile back and had followed it a couple of miles before realizing his mistake. He was relieved to see us, and his gratitude was our reward. I knew without really knowing much about him, except that he was a backpacker, that he would have done the same for me.

In a similar way, if someone ran short of food, we delved into our food bags and shared what surplus we had. Within minutes, the famished hiker would find himself stationed before a mountain of Ziploc bags of rice and noodles. And, if someone turned an ankle and twisted a knee, we carried some of the weight from his pack until his injury healed. Victor, an upbeat man in his early twenties from Northampton, Massachusetts, who had linked up with Dan and me in Georgia, pulled a calf muscle the day we entered the Smokies. As we moved north and Victor's limp became more and more conspicuous, we volunteered to carry some of his weight. When he refused, we insisted. Unfortunately, our help was not enough, and Victor then wrestled with the decision to abandon the trail.

When Victor seemed to have reached his limit, we encouraged him to plod on, and, in spite of his injury, he continued on to Hot Springs, North Carolina, thirty-five miles north of the Smokies. Realizing that, if he continued, he would just slow us down, he bought a bus ticket home. When he departed the trail, we embraced him and wished him well, and, for days afterward, we felt that an important part of our family was absent. The separation proved to be only temporary, however. Months later, when we entered New England, Victor rejoined us for weekends and accompanied us for the final 120 miles of the trail.

Though most hikers shared the same experiences, we were all different in terms of ages, backgrounds, and regions of the country. One night at Muskrat Creek Shelter, three miles beyond the North Carolina–Georgia line, I shared the shelter with a sixty-five-year-old mathematics professor from Ottawa, who had navigated a mountain bike loaded with bulging panniers to the shelter; a seventy-two-year-old retired Army sergeant and veteran of World War II and Korea; two tattooed heavy-metal mavens in their early twenties from northern Kentucky; and a clean-cut twenty-six-year-old butcher from Washington, D.C. It occurred to me that, if we had met under any other circumstances, we probably would not have had much to talk about. We had all arrived at the A-frame shelter after walking through a driving thunderstorm, and, although we were virtual strangers, we spent the evening packed under a ten-by-twelve-foot roof, discussing religion, philosophy, and our personal reasons for being on the trail, while swapping samples from our cook pots. At bedtime, we slithered into our sleeping bags in the dank shelter illuminated by a single candle, and, as the rain peppered the roof, someone told a joke, then another, and another. For more than an hour, we lay awake listening and laughing together. The barriers of age, education, and social status couldn't have mattered less.

A couple of hundred miles farther north, at Cherry Gap Shelter, a day's hike south of Roan Mountain in the northeastern corner of Tennessee, we had a similar experience. It was May 24. We had been on the trail for just over a month, and the continuing warming of spring had inspired Dan and me to ship our woolens, gloves, and heavy sweaters home from the town of Erwin, believing that we had suffered winter's last blast. We were mistaken.

Dan and I began shivering soon after we arrived in camp that afternoon. The temperatures during the day had lingered in the sixties and seventies—too warm to induce shivering—and so we ascribed our chills to the flu-like effects of bad water. By dusk, however, we realized that the air temperature had dropped more than thirty degrees. The next morning, we awoke to two inches of snow. It blanketed the ground and bowed the trees, now in full summer foliage. As we prepared to leave the shelter, a combination of snow and sleet began to fall, and we abandoned our travel plans for the day. We spent the morning hours drinking herbal tea and reading, and, by noon, the first of our benumbed colleagues began to arrive. Some of them had slept under ponchos through the night's storm. By midafternoon, eleven hikers were wedged into a shelter designed to sleep six, and only by alternating head to foot could we squeeze everyone in.

Nestled in our sleeping bags, we read our books, wrote in our journals, munched surplus food, or stared out into the icy woods. Someone passed around a plastic bottle filled with Jack Daniel's, and, by dusk, we were one very happy family. Through the evening hours, we sang verses of a blues song, creating new verses as we progressed, and joking about the wicked weather, the flatulence that resulted from our heavy dietary regimen of legumes, our ailing feet, or the wild stench that rose from eleven filthy, pressure-packed bodies. What had the makings for a bad scene still endures among my most cherished memories of the trail. It was a prime example of making do with what nature throws your way and finding contentment in companionship and simple pleasures.

If there was any sense of isolation from being on the trail for months at a time, it was isolation from world and national news.

We spent from three to ten days at a stretch between resupply trips to town. We didn't carry radios, and, during our stopovers, we rarely picked up newspapers. Frankly, there wasn't much going on in the world that interested us. The big news during the summer of 1979, for instance, was the gas shortage and the fuel-rationing programs in effect in major cities. We heard stories about escalating gas prices, long lines at the pump, and the occasional shooting that resulted when someone edged his way into line. To us, the gas crunch meant only one thing: By the end of the summer, it cost us eight, rather than six, cents to fill our fuel bottles.

Much more important to us was the latest trail news. We gleaned most of this news from the spiral notebooks left in many of the trail shelters. On these pages, hikers signed in, mentioned the highlights or low points of their days, described the weather, listed the other hikers in their parties, drew caricatures of themselves, and sometimes waxed philosophical about the vicissitudes of life on the trail.

Through the summer, we followed the exploits of other thru-hikers: Otel (who, according to rumor, sometimes hiked in the buff) and his dog A.T.; Al and Moonie, a couple of good-natured cut-ups from New Jersey; the Phillips brothers, Paul and Robin, two siblings from Florida who packed heavy photographic equipment; Woodstock and Nancy and Phil and Cindy, two of the trail's few man-woman teams; Byron and Jimmy—Byron, who had a ready joke for every occasion and who eventually lost his pack to a trailside thief; and Jimmy, who recorded humorous and bawdy trail tales in the registers. On later trips to the trail, I followed Sunshine and Daydream, a newlywed couple from Connecticut; Captain Kangaroo, an Australian hiker who became a friend; Pigpen, an accountant from Boston who refused to bathe; the Bluegrass Boys, a trio of hikers from northern Kentucky.

Through register entries, we came to know each of the hikers who plodded along anywhere from a few hours to days and weeks ahead of us before we even met them. We learned of their likes and dislikes, the types of food that filled their bellies, their struggles, their triumphs, the professions they had left to hike the trail, and even what they looked like, the styles of packs they carried, and what they wore. When we caught up with them, we could call them by name before they had a chance to introduce themselves, just as the hikers behind us would often come into camp and without hesitation announce, "You must be Dan and Dave. I've been on your heels for two weeks."

We often used the registers to communicate messages to those behind us, urging them to hustle to catch us for a beer bash or a megafeed at a town stop, or telling them, sadly, when someone in our party had reached his limit and had gone home. At times, the efficiency of our primitive communications network amazed us. Near the end of June, for instance, Dan and I approached Harpers Ferry, West Virginia, headquarters for the Appalachian Trail Conference and the unofficial halfway point. As we progressed north, we left a series of entries inviting other thru-hikers to hitchhike the fifty miles from Harpers Ferry into Washington, D.C., for the Fourth of July celebration on the Mall. We planned to meet at noon at the Jefferson Memorial.

By noon on the fourth, nearly a dozen hikers—many of whom we had never met—straggled to the memorial. We spent the afternoon swapping trail stories and enjoying the bounty of junk food available from sidewalk vendors.

Southbounders on the trail—those who had begun their hike in Maine rather than Georgia—became another source of trail news. When we encountered them, we often slipped from our packs and shared a bag of trail mix while we exchanged data. Our news was as vital to them as theirs was to us; each could provide the other with information about what lay ahead: the friendliest towns, the cheapest hotels and restaurants, the most taxing ascents and descents, the locations of reliable water sources.

Through the summer, we leapfrogged with dozens of other northbounders who had left Springer about the same time we had. Among them were the Phillips brothers, Jeff Hammons from Kansas, North Carolina native Gary Owen, and Mark Gornick from Maryland. We would link up with them for several days, or even weeks, losing them after we or they had stopped for an extended stay in one place. Two or three months later, we would catch them at a shelter farther north and spend hours around the campfire, detailing the important events of our lives and discussing how we had changed.

In terms of our appearance, the changes were obvious. One night in Maine, I rejoined Al, a solitary hiker from New York whom we had last seen in Hot Springs, North Carolina. Al had adopted a mongrel dog he had found near Wayah Bald in North Carolina and had named the animal Wayah. Wayah had contracted a bad case of mange, and, as Dan and I left Hot Springs, Wayah—completely bereft of fur—lay wheezing in the grass. Both Dan and I wrote her off as a lost cause.

Yet, some four months later, Al and Wayah, the latter sporting a luxurious new coat of fur, entered camp. We laughed at Wayah's changed appearance, and Al laughed at ours. Al, who had started the hike with a billowy beard, really hadn't changed much, but we had. I had started the trail with a haircut, a clean-shaven face, ten pounds of unwanted fat, and a crisp, new hiking outfit. I had long ago surrendered my threadbare khakis and now wore a pair of tattered fatigue trousers with holes in the knees and seat. My beard had grown to three inches, and I had hardened, having lost the ten pounds.

LTHOUGH THE TRAIL PROVIDED AN AMPLE MEASURE of male companionship, during my five months in the wilderness, I suffered a pestering hunger for the physical affection of a woman. Along the trail, when virtually all of one's sensibilities became attuned to sensual cues and when one spent his days surrounded by beauty, peace, and harmony, it seemed natural to hunger for touch and to surrender, like most of nature's creatures, to the attraction of members of the opposite sex. The problem was that the pickings were slim.

Though the ratio of men to women is becoming more balanced each year, in 1979, we met fewer than ten women who aspired to complete the trail. If we did want to meet women, it seemed, we would have to create them in our own imaginations, which we often did. One night over a few ounces of bourbon by a campfire, Dan and I created mythological Venuses we dubbed the "Scandinavian hiking queens." In our minds, they were beautiful, lithesome women who would love us, share our experiences, and provide feminine companionship. They became the object of our hormone-inspired quest, although neither one of us ever imagined we actually would encounter them in the flesh. Against the odds, in the White Mountains of New Hampshire, I met a woman who more than matched my fantasy.

The White Mountains, for all their stark, alpine beauty, also tend to attract throngs of hiking enthusiasts, which for us created nightly contests for shelter space. On August 29, we had left Garfield Ridge Campsite and, in a cold New England rain, pushed on toward Ethan Pond, a campsite that included a six-man shelter and several tent platforms. Though none of us wanted to acknowledge concern over finding shelter space for the night—to have done so would have smacked of the competitiveness we had shunned in greater society—the rain inspired a quickening of our pace, and each of us discreetly counted heads and jockeyed for position over the last few miles to the pond, lest we be left out in the rain.

By that stage of the trip, my rain fly, which had served as a groundsheet as often as a shelter, bore visible holes and admitted almost as much rain as it repelled. I didn't want to suffer a cold, clammy night beneath it.

When we arrived at Ethan Pond Campsite, we encountered six sullen faces peering out of the shelter into the rain. Dan managed to secure a space in the shelter after persuading a reluctant weekender to shift his body, along with his staggering assemblage of gear, over a few inches. If the shelter had been full of thru-hikers, I have no doubt they would have accommodated me, too, but weekenders were notoriously protective of their personal space, and there clearly was no room for me.

I walked out to the tent platform, a ten-by-ten-foot elevated square of rain-soaked wooden slats, and began erecting my pitiful shelter. The task proved counterproductive in the rain, so I decided to wait to see if the rain would quit and walked back to dump my pack under the shelter's eaves. A while later, feeling crowded, I left the shelter and returned to the tent platform, somewhat reconciled to the notion that it would be my home for the night. Nearby, I noticed a large olive-drab tent mounted on another platform.

Just outside the tent, I met its occupant, a friendly, long-legged woman with brown hair topped by a blue wool watch cap. I eyed her ample shelter, and, without presuming to ask if there was room inside for an extra boarder, I began complaining about my leaky digs for the night. Sensing my misery, she asked me to join her for a cup of hot tea inside the tent.

A large gas stove had heated the tent to a comfortable seventy degrees, and a steaming kettle sat on the burner. From it, she poured two cups of herbal tea, and, as we sipped our drinks, we talked about her frequent trips to the White Mountains and about my experiences along the trail. She was a bright, cheerful woman whose knowledge of the wilderness amazed me. At dusk, I rose to leave, but she seemed to sense my reluctance and asked if I'd like to stay the night in her tent. Without hesitating, I accepted her offer.

After we had finished our dinners, we sat close to a candle, and she showed me clippings from many of the edible plants that grew in the area: wood sorrel, a tart, tri-leaved plant that resembles clover and provides vitamin C; reindeer moss, a fungus of light green, skeletal tines that boasts a musky mushroom flavor; and Labrador tea leaves, taken from a low-growing evergreen heath, which she steeped in boiling water and served to me with honey.

As we sat close over the candle, I wanted to move closer, to smell her hair, to kiss her. I wanted to hold her, not necessarily make love to her, but just hold her. For all of its gifts, the trail deprived us of that one thing—touch—which I believe we all craved. As we prepared to climb into our bags, I gently touched her back, and she drew away from me. I apologized and backed away, explaining how lonely for affection I had grown over the past few months and how much I enjoyed her company.

Moments later, with the candle out, I heard her slip from her clothes and enter her bag. I, too, lay naked in mine. Then, I felt her hand reach for mine, and, for an hour, we lay silent, just stroking one another's hands. I reached over and kissed her, and she took me in her arms, kissing me back. Soon, we had rearranged our bags, laying one on the tent floor and covering ourselves with the other. We kissed and embraced through the night, sleeping and awakening in each other's arms, never making love but succumbing to blissful, innocent intimacy.

Near dawn, she suggested that we walk outside to experience the cold rain against our skin, then return to the warmth of our sleeping bags. We did, and we ran naked and barefoot through the rain along the trail. Back in the tent, we climbed under our sleeping bags, still warm from when we had left them, and fell asleep. Soon, in spite of my desire to prolong the night forever, it was morning.

Over breakfast, she asked me if I would like some company for the morning hike. Yes, I told her, and, in a dramatic overture that might have been lifted from a grade-B romance movie, I suggested that she accompany me to Katahdin. She hugged me, laughing at the suggestion. Once I realized how ridiculous it must have sounded, I laughed, too. I realized I was falling in love; all relationships, it seems, develop rapidly in the rarefied environment of the trail.

Together, we left Ethan Pond and descended into Crawford Notch. As we began the long, three-mile ascent to the Presidential Range, the sun emerged, and the temperature rose. Midway up the climb, she stopped me and asked if I would be offended if she hiked topless, explaining that she didn't want to sweat in her last clean T-shirt. I hiked shirtless, so it seemed natural for her to do the same.

Besides, how could I pass up a chance to view her beautiful body in the daylight? She pulled her shirt off and slipped back into her pack, and we continued up the trail.

From time to time, as we ascended, I glanced back at her and admired her body moving sensuously with her stride. I was struck by how her natural beauty complemented that of the wilderness.

As we neared the ridge, I spotted one of my fellow hikers, a quiet, contemplative Connecticut native whose face displayed little emotion—that is, until the day he caught a glimpse of a beautiful, topless woman bounding up the trail. The hiker, who sat on a rock munching trail mix, looked up, spotted me, nodded a silent hello, and returned his glance to the bag of trail mix on his lap. When his glance rose again, my hiking partner had come into view, and his eyes beamed like dual harvest moons. As we passed, the hiker, always a man of few words, was stunned totally speechless.

My friend left me at the Mizpah Hut, six miles short of Lakes of the Clouds Hut, our destination for the day. For the rest of the trip, I replayed our night together often in my mind as I walked alone through the woods, and I savor the memory even now. As it was, it was a perfect union of two free-spirited souls—a man and a woman—both searching for some meaning in the eastern wilderness and finding unexpected intimacy. If it had lasted longer, it might have lost some of its intensity. If it had not lasted as long, I would have regretted every second that was lost.

When I think of her, I recall of a line from Whitman's "I Sing the Body Electric":

> I have perceived that to be with those I like is
>   enough,
> To stop in company with the rest at evening is
>   enough,
> To be surrounded by beautiful, curious, breathing,
>   laughing flesh is enough…

CHAPTER SIX

Bad Company

We had our first encounter with lowlifes last night at Roan Highlands Shelter. A couple of gun-toting hoodlums in leather jackets and a drunken woman had hiked the half-mile from the road, and they commandeered the shelter for their private party. Only the Phillips brothers were bold enough to demand space inside. The rest of us were content to sleep in our tents.

A couple of weeks ago, we heard a hiker tell a story about being abducted at a road crossing by some locals in a pick-up truck. Apparently, they demanded that he help them rob other people or that he would himself become their victim. He was able to escape when the truck stopped at a backwoods road junction, as a car just happened to pass. He leaped from the truck, grabbed his pack, and ran into the woods. They searched for him for a few minutes, and he escaped unharmed. We've also heard stories from other hikers about moonshiners at backwoods road crossings who offer to sell them hooch. Seems that such encounters take place where roads intrude into the wilderness. Not much good results when their world and ours collide. Even in the face of such risk, I feel much safer out here on the trail than I would in any major city.

MAY 26, 1979

ROAN HIGHLANDS SHELTER, TENNESSEE

IT WAS A SUNDAY EVENING IN THE EARLY SPRING 1987, and I shared Addis Gap Shelter in Georgia with a married couple, Kit and Candy, and their pit bull, A.T.

As we arrived at camp, the sun dipped behind the ridge. We quickly unrolled our bags and dressed in our camp clothes, ready to settle in for the night and enjoy the tranquil setting that had once been the site of the Addis family homestead. A grove of Carolina silver-bell trees sprinkled the ground with delicate white blossoms shaken free by the breeze. The slanting rays of the sun traced long shadows across the clearing, and a small brook sluiced away from the shelter down a hillside. Amid all the beauty, however, there was one unsettling feature: a gravel forest service road that wound up the mountain came within a few hundred feet of the shelter.

Most hikers have learned to apply the following postulate to their wilderness wanderings: The quality of people increases in proportion to the distance from the nearest road and the difficulty of the terrain. In other words, the bad guys don't have the gumption or stamina to hump heavy packs into the heart of the backcountry.

Service roads linked the backcountry with the outer world and invited intrusion, and occasionally they attracted an often belligerent corps of locals who drove their fat-tired 4x4s up into the mountains to fire their guns, drink beer, and sometimes harass foot travelers. Often such backwoods crossings were choked with discarded trash, littered with spent shotgun shells and empty whiskey and beer bottles, and gutted by all-terrain vehicles. We needed only to view the scattered refuse to know that our nemeses had been there, and we could only hope that our arrival would not coincide with theirs. I can't speak for other hikers, but I know that I always tensed when I approached such crossings, realizing that if I did emerge from the woods and face trouble, there wasn't much I could do to defend myself.

In all my days in the woods, I met only one hiker who had stowed a weapon in his pack. The rest of us felt that to walk armed would violate the true spirit of the trail. It also would have violated the law against carrying concealed weapons in national parks and forests. Besides, in view of our preoccupation with cutting weight, it would have been unconscionable to supplant one pound of food with one pound of steel.

During our night at Addis Gap, the road brought unwelcome visitors. As the three of us sparked our stoves and set about cooking our dinners, we heard a vehicle approach.

"That had better be a government truck," Kit said.

I hoped so, too, but realized that it probably wasn't. It was Sunday, late in the day. By that time, most government employees were off the clock. Then, we heard a volley of gunfire echo through the woods, which resolved any doubt.

A brown pick-up truck soon rounded a bend and came into view. From the distance of several hundred yards, I noticed that the cab carried four people. As the vehicle drew nearer, I saw that it contained two men and two women. The truck continued until it reached the end of the road, thirty yards behind the shelter. Now out of our sight, the driver killed the engine. We heard the doors swing open.

"Oh, shit," I said under my breath. "We've got company." I heard the two women giggling like adolescents. One of the men cursed them, telling them to shut up.

The four then stepped around to the front of the shelter. The two women—plump and in their midthirties, dressed in double-knit shorts and halter tops—stayed in the background giggling, while the men took seats at the picnic table perched in front of the shelter. I expected the protective pit bull to charge over my shoulder and confront the men, but I peered behind me—amazed—to find her snoozing peacefully at the back of the shelter.

The two men held beers in their hands and reeked of alcohol. The tall, gaunt man with dark eyes, a black beard, and stringy, shoulder-length hair, glared into the shelter for a time before he spoke.

"You know these shelters are for everyone," he said, sternly. Then, he smiled at his friend, a portly man with red hair and bloodshot eyes. The man smiled back. "They're not just for you backpackers."

We told him we knew that.

"Most hikers think they own these places," he continued, "but it ain't that way."

"Y'all want something to drink?" asked the friend, still wearing a queer smile. "We got some liquor and some beer. Done smoked up the pot, though."

There was a fresh ripple of giggling from the women.

"No, that's okay, but thanks," I answered.

"Naw y'all gonna drink a beer," commanded the dark-haired man.

His friend returned to the truck. I suspected he might return with the beer and a weapon. While he was gone, his dark friend glared into the shelter at us without talking. I'm sure our apprehension was palpable. The redheaded man soon returned, proffering two beers.

As the women continued to giggle, the dark man snapped to his friend, "Hell, we ought to take them two out and shoot them!"

The redheaded man laughed, and I tried to muster a smile but couldn't. I knew that it was unlikely that the man would make good on his threat, but there was always a chance. These mountains were thoroughly isolated from the law.

The men stayed for nearly an hour, without talking much, but just glaring into the shelter. The pit bull continued to sleep. As night fell, they discussed staying at the shelter but finally decided to move on, saying they might be back later with some friends.

Relieved, we watched the truck wind away down the road and disappear around the bend.

"Think they were trying to scare us?" I asked.

"Well, they succeeded," Kit answered.

We discussed whether to move on up the trail or stay in the shelter and risk facing the men and a group of their hiker-hating allies later in the night.

Then, we heard the truck stop and the doors open. Two shots rang through the trees, rousing the pit bull, who sat bolt upright, growling.

There was no need for further discussion. Quickly, we were all on our feet, frantically stowing our gear. Within ten minutes, we were racing north on the trail through the darkness. We spent a restless night on a mountain shoulder half a mile beyond the shelter, and I awoke several times through the night to hear the pit bull, tensed and alert, growling at shadows in the woods. From where we lay, I spotted a string of lights marking faraway backwoods houses extending down through the valley, and, in my sleepy daze, I imagined a pack of militant locals stalking us through the woods with flashlights.

Eight years earlier and a few hundred miles farther north, I had confronted another weapon-toting yokel, not on the trail but in Erwin, a small trail town in northern Tennessee. Because of intolerance for hikers among some of the town's residents, in the late 1970s, Erwin ranked as one of the trail's least hospitable stopovers. Erwin's most enduring legacy it seems involves the lynching of an elephant some years ago. As the story goes, during a circus in a nearby town, an elephant squashed a young spectator, and, after a brief trial, the town hired a crane operator in Erwin, who summarily executed the hapless creature by hanging.

Over the last decade, the town has made great strides to clean up its reputation. The Nolichucky Retreat Campground and

Nolichucky Expeditions, a rafting outfitter located on the banks of the Nolichucky River now offer hikers comfortable and friendly accommodations. But, in 1979, in some ways, Erwin seemed almost as inhospitable to hikers as it had been to clumsy pachyderms.

After we arrived in town, we found our way to the YMCA, a dingy edifice, and we welcomed the chance to take a hot shower and sleep under a roof, such as it was.

The shelters we had passed on our approach to town had posted warnings to hikers advising them not to interact with locals and not to divulge their travel plans. The signs made it clear that there had been trouble with some of the people from the area.

Though the town offered us little in the way of amenities, it was the first "wet" town we had passed through in many days, and, after dropping our packs at the Y, Dan and I walked to one of the town's few taverns, several streets away. The tavern was nothing more than a long, dimly lit room with a chipped linoleum floor, a row of rickety stools, and a large cooler filled with iced quarts of Iron City Beer. Seventy-five cents bought a quart of beer and a styrofoam cup.

As soon as we crossed the threshold, I realized that we had made a mistake. Fifteen bleary-eyed patrons swung their faces toward the door, and, as they did, conversation ceased. Most of the men wore work shirts and billed caps advertising chewing tobacco, fishing gear, or four-wheel-drive trucks. Some of the men had wads of tobacco bulging in their cheeks and sluiced the juice right onto the floor.

Clad in our hiking clothes and boots and with our long hair and beards—both emblems of the counterculture in 1979—we made ready targets. The men recognized us immediately as hikers or, worse, as hippie hikers who had chucked the work ethic to wander through the woods. Their values and ours, at least as they perceived them, were at odds, and I confess that I, too, was guilty of making snap judgments about the men and their attitudes toward us. It turned out that my snap judgments weren't too far off.

Dan and I sidled up to the bar, ordered the house specialty, and soon sat in front of two frothy styrofoam cups.

"Hey, what the hell you fellows doin' walking when you can drive!" said one of the men. Laughter. "Wall, look at 'em boots! 'Em's some fancy boots!" More laughter. "You all walk in 'em cute little shorts?" Again, more laughter. I noticed that Dan's beer had vanished in one quaff, and he fixed me with a look that said, "Let's get the hell out of here. Now."

I took a long pull at my beer, hoping that the onslaught would end and that the men would focus their attention on something else. They didn't. The man on my left, who tottered unsteadily on his perch, turned a red, haggard face toward me and started raving about something. I'm sure he had a definite message in mind, but, under the influence of a few dozen beers, all that came out was a string of garbled syllables. From the few words I could understand, I learned that the man was angry with a fellow named Rufus or Verl or some such, who had taken liberties with his daughter.

About that time, he rested his elbow on my shoulder and reached his free hand into his work pants and pulled out a small silver handgun.

I had had a terrifying experience in college when, at a barn dance, a drunken lunatic who had infiltrated the college crowd pulled a western-style revolver, poked it into my chest, pushed me back, and leveled the gun at my heart before someone wrestled the weapon from his hand. The experience left me with a dread of handguns.

Now, in this dingy Tennessee tavern, as the sodden man waved the loaded gun in my face, I felt a twinge of panic. I looked at Dan, and, for the first time since I'd known him, I saw he was frightened.

The man continued to bellow about this Rufus and how he was going to "kill that son of a bitch," when the man seated on his left intervened.

"Jack, you can't kill Rufus," he said. "He hanged hisself in prison last week!"

With his primary target gone, I imagined that the man might

turn his sights on me. At that, Dan rose, sensibly figuring that this was an appropriate time to leave.

Just then, our savior—a disabled young man with a vacant smile—entered the bar. He was, in the lexicon of this rural hamlet, the reigning village idiot, and the tavern denizens aimed their abuse at him. They jeered him and mocked him, but his smile indicated that he enjoyed the attention, derisive though it was.

The man's presence seemed to boost Jack's mood, and he called the crippled man over to the bar. As the young man approached, Jack pulled the clip from his gun and withdrew a single 22-caliber round. He then told the man that he had a game he could play, and he demonstrated how to pound the butt-end of the cartridge against the sharp metal edge of the bar with the slug pointed at his head. He handed the bullet to the man and backed away. As he did, Dan and I made our way toward the door.

My last memory of the tavern was of the pathetic man, the silly grin still playing across his face, pounding the bullet against the edge of the bar while the men stood clear of danger, laughing and waiting for the round to discharge.

Within a week, on May 26, at the Roan Highlands Shelter in Low Gap, four miles north of the summit of Roan Mountain, we had another bizarre encounter. Six of us—the Phillips brothers; Mark, an eighteen-year-old thru-hiker from Maryland; Jeff, a Kansas native; and Dan and I—arrived at the shelter as it began to drizzle. Inside were two rough-looking men clad in black leather jackets who had hiked in the half-mile from the nearest road. With them was an attractive woman with long dark hair and brown eyes. She and the men swilled whiskey from a Jack Daniel's bottle that sat on the floor beside a healthy store of tin cans.

The men seemed irked at our arrival, and they made it clear that they planned on making good use of the shelter that night and did not welcome our company. The woman, though drunk, seemed happy enough with her two companions.

Most of us decided to avoid a confrontation and set up our tents and rain flies outside the shelter. The Phillips brothers, nonetheless, determined to wedge their way into the shelter, and, after a few minutes of tense negotiation, the men grudgingly yielded. To ensure their privacy, the men hung two rain ponchos from the shelter eaves, one dividing the shelter in half, and the other closing off the front.

Through the evening, as we huddled around a smoky fire, the three continued to party. At one point, we dived for cover when we heard one of the men shout at the woman to put down the gun. Having discovered that the men were armed, we spent a restless night inside our nylon tents. The next morning, we were packed and on the trail before the hung-over revelers awoke, and, as we walked, the Phillips brothers shared what they had overheard from beyond the nylon partition.

"One of the men had sex with the woman a couple of times, and then he called his friend over," he said. "He told the girl that he wanted her to have sex with his friend." The woman, who was all but comatose at that point, initially resisted but then accommodated the man's request. The men apparently took turns with her through the night.

As we distanced ourselves from the shelter, we wrestled with our judgment, wondering if we should have intervened in the woman's behalf. After some discussion, we decided we had done the right thing. The woman seemed to be a willing participant, and, if we had intervened, what would the outcome have been if we had confronted the two burly, armed men in defense of a woman whose honor seemed as dubious as theirs?

 HE GUN-WIELDING ROGUES WERE INTIMIDATING, but even they did not rattle us nearly as much as the illusive nocturnal demon that sent us fleeing from the shore of Tiorati Lake forty miles outside of New York City.

It was July 30, and I was traveling with Paul. Dan had pushed a day ahead, and Nick lagged a few days behind. We had veered off the trail ten miles south of Bear Mountain Bridge, where the trail crosses the Hudson River, and, at dusk, we found ourselves following the paved roads through Tiorati Circle.

At that point, we had become thoroughly at ease in the wilderness, yet the prospect of mixing with the denizens of the nation's largest city, which lay a scant forty miles away, left us spooked.

Initially, Paul and I had decided to camp on Tiorati Circle, a paved loop a few yards off the trail that ran along the shores of Tiorati Lake Resort. When we got there, we encountered riotous commotion that left us feeling like back-country immigrants newly arrived in a society devoted to noise, hedonism, and excess. One camper, a plump man in his early thirties, sat in a lawn chair basking in the glow of a Coleman lantern beside a small card table cluttered with a three-foot water pipe for smoking pot, a quart bottle of whiskey, and a massive sound system that blared disco dance music. In the site beside his, a family outfitted with an equally outsized boom-box blasted their hard-rock strains into the night. Several young men in souped-up cars had converted the circle into a racetrack, and they sped around the oval squealing their tires, shouting to other drivers and blaring their own music through open windows.

At the outset of my hike, I would have welcomed the security of having other campers—even such boisterous ones—gathered around me, but the three months on the trail had changed my perspective. These disrespectful urban campers seemed to violate the peaceful sanctity of the wilderness while they violated my own peace of mind, and Paul and I wanted nothing to do with them.

Before making camp, we decided to push up the road to find a less frenetic setting, even though it was now dark. Within a half-mile, we passed a group camp area where a dozen inner-city children—most of them from Harlem—sat clustered around a campfire grilling hot dogs and hamburgers. The delicious aroma of cooking meat tempered our wariness, and we ambled over to the fire. Soon, we sat swapping tales with the children while sharing their dinner. Just before we left, a raccoon wandered into the camp, and the children scattered, screaming, from the fire. One young boy shrieked, "Bear! It's a bear!" as he ran.

Paul and I couldn't help but laugh at the irony. These kids had grown up on some of the meanest streets in America, where they had no doubt witnessed muggings, shootings, stabbings, and other violent crimes. Yet, to them, the wilderness and its harmless creatures were unfamiliar and strange, evoking fear and panic. A dozen armed gang members could have wandered into camp and not raised an eye-brow, but a ten-pound raccoon sent the children fleeing for their lives.

Paul and I thanked the children and their counselors for the kindness and pushed on. Faced with the prospect of bumbling through the brush in the dark looking for a suitable place to sleep, we opted instead to take our chances amid the noise and confusion back at Tiorati Circle.

We rolled out our bags along the fringes of the lake and decided not to hang our food, convinced that the noise from our neighbors would at least protect us from scavenging animals.

Minutes after we had climbed into our bags, we heard the horrible call. It wouldn't have been more unsettling if it had risen from the throat of a Godzilla. Instead, it was the call of the dread *homo sapiens intoxicatus*, and it came from the campsite nearest ours.

"Ahhhhhhh!" it began. "Ahhhhhhhhhh! Somebody stole my friggin' radio!"

Seconds later, a dark form was crashing through the bushes, and soon a bearded man in a white T-shirt and ball cap tottered above us as we cowered in our sleeping bags.

"I'm gonna kill the son of a bitch who stole my radio!" he shouted in our direction. "Yoos guys seen my radio?"

No, we explained, we hadn't. But, we'd be sure to keep an eye out for it.

After scanning our spartan camp, he seemed convinced of our innocence and staggered on through the weeds toward the next site. "Ahhhhhhhhhhh! Somebody stole my friggin' radio! I'm gonna kill the bastard who stole my radio."

Serenaded by the squealing tires, blaring music, and the mournful call of the radio-less man, we eventually fell asleep. But, the urban reign of terror wasn't over for us quite yet.

About 3:00 a.m., after even the most devoted partyers had drifted off, I heard it. I shook Paul in his bag.

"Listen," I said.

It was the sound of something large, plunging with its paws and splashing through the water of the lake. It was moving toward our camp.

"What is it?" Paul asked.

"God, I don't know," I continued, "but I think we ought to hang our food."

Still half asleep, we slipped from our bags, and I fumbled through my pack for the fifty feet of parachute cord I carried for hanging our food. As I did, I could hear the strange creature plunging through the water toward us. I found the rope and, as Paul fixed his flashlight beam on a branch above us, tied a rock to one end of the rope before hurling it toward the branch. It missed. As I felt along the ground for the rope, Paul swung his flashlight toward the advancing creature.

"I can't see anything, but it's still moving toward us," he said.

"Yeah, and we'd better get this food up before it gets here," I said.

Before I could take another shot at the branch, the creature had cleared the shoreline and began moving through the brush.

I'm not sure if it was my imagination, but I swear I could see the whites of Paul's eyes bulging, and, before I could stop him, he tore off through the trees in the opposite direction. Not one to face peril alone, I followed on his heels, and together we charged willy-nilly through the woods, peering over our shoulders to glimpse the mystery predator. Although we couldn't see what or who pursued us, we could hear it rustling through the brush a constant fifteen yards behind us, matching us stride for stride.

At one point, I grabbed Paul's arm, and we stopped to listen. As soon as we stopped, the creature stopped. After a few seconds, we spooked again and sped off, howling through the trees. The creature again was on our heels, fifteen yards behind us. I spotted the light of the bathhouse and raced toward it, thinking that we'd finally get a good look at our pursuer.

When we arrived under the light, we peered behind us. Still nothing. Then, I cast a glance down at my boot and started laughing.

"What's so funny?" Paul asked.

"We are," I answered. "Look at my boot."

Looking down, he saw the parachute cord tangled around my ankle and started laughing too. I had been dragging the parachute cord through the weeds, and we had been fleeing from the dread rock monster I had secured to the other end while I was trying to hang our food bags. We may have identified one of our assailants, but the other, the bizarre aquatic demon that had plunged through the water toward our camp, remains a mystery.

CHAPTER SEVEN

Sheep and Wolves

No matter how poorly prepared I feel for this trip, there is always someone less prepared, less well equipped, less conditioned. Some of the people out here are like harlequins in hiking boots. Some have never read a single word about this trail or hiked a single mile before setting out, and their misadventures tend to encourage me. Compared with some of them, I am a virtual expert on backwoods living. I've discovered, too, that there are a few con men out here, who seem to be preying on them.

MAY 5, 1979
FONTANA DAM, NORTH CAROLINA

 WHITE GAUZE BANDAGE CRUSTED WITH A YELLOW stain clung to Mark's forehead, a reminder of his rather inauspicious introduction to the Appalachian Trail. His eyes, glazed and distant, peered lifelessly from their sockets.

He curled in his cotton-flannel sleeping bag in the recesses of the Springer Mountain Shelter, staring blankly out into the greening, rain-drenched forest while his hiking partner, Don, a tiny man who stood five feet tall and weighed 105 pounds, set about building a fire. Don may have been small, but he was mightily armed. A massive hunting knife—a machete, really—hung from his belt and extended below his knee. In his right hand, he held a full-sized axe, which he wielded fiercely against the unyielding trunk of a very large and healthy maple.

After assaulting the trunk for several minutes with no results, he lowered the axe. Wheezing like an asthmatic, he scanned the woods for a more accommodating target, locating a smaller, though no less healthy, green maple. Straining to bend the small tree nearly double and struggling to secure the top to the ground with his foot, he grunted as he drove the axe into the midsection. The axe head rebounded like a Superball and struck Don square in the forehead, knocking him to his knees.

"Oh, shit," muttered Mark. "Now this."

The two of them were not having a good day. In fact, it had been a pretty miserable week. Only a few days earlier, Don and he had had high hopes for their journey on the Appalachian Trail. They had been planning for weeks, organizing their equipment, purchasing food, sharpening their axes and knives. But, things hadn't worked out the way they had hoped, and their dreams, along with Mark's head—and now Don's—had been dashed.

Mark's head injury had occurred before they even reached the trail. After becoming entangled in his pack straps, Mark had stumbled off the bus that had carried them to Atlanta and had landed solidly on his forehead. The ambulance ride to the emergency room was an unexpected side trip, but Mark was relieved when the doctor glanced at the X-rays and reported that he had not fractured his skull. He had, however, suffered a wicked concussion, which had left him dazed and confused, and the medication they had given him to quiet his nerves had only compounded the problem. Against the doctor's orders, he had checked out of the hospital two days later. After purchasing two twelve-packs of Budweiser, Mark and Don had set out for Amicalola Falls.

The eight-and-a-half-mile hike up from the falls to the official start of the Appalachian Trail hadn't exactly met their expectations, either. Neither had trained for the hike, and the stiff uphill grade soon exhausted them. It also made them thirsty. They hadn't bothered to fill their canteens with water before leaving the park. Why bother? Each carried 144 ounces of beer, and, as they struggled up the mountain, they left a trail of empty twelve-ounce aluminum cans behind them.

Near the halfway point, Mark began to suffer another spell. His vision blurred, and he spun and collapsed into a heap beside the trail. After Don assessed the situation, he became convinced that his partner was dehydrated and decided to go for water. Had they carried a map or guidebook, they would have realized that a perfectly good spring spouted water within a few hundred yards of their emergency bivouac, but the twelve cans of beer had already made their packs unmanageably heavy, and they had left the trail guide behind.

As his partner lapsed deeper into a daze, Don humped the four miles to the top of Springer Mountain, located the spring at the shelter, filled his canteen, then spun back down the mountain to his friend. By the time Don returned, Mark was sitting up, cradling his throbbing head. By now, it was dark, and the two rolled out their sleeping bags—heavy cotton-flannel models—in the brush and tried to ignore the rain that pummeled their faces and drenched their bags. It seems they had also neglected to bring a tent.

That was the end of day one.

The next morning, the two arose. Don arose, rather, while Mark, pale and wan, lay in his bag, his lifeless eyes cast toward the heavens. Don revived him with a tepid Budweiser, and, after a breakfast of Fig Newtons, the two once again embarked for Springer more determined than ever.

Late that afternoon, long after they had exhausted their cache of beer, they arrived at the shelter, Mark tottering unsteadily and Don dragging his sodden sleeping bag behind him like a thick serpentine tail. While Mark lay in the shelter, his partner set out to build a fire to warm them and dry their wet clothes. Since no dead trees lay within two hundred yards of the shelter, in the interest of convenience, he opted to fell a few live ones, which was not proceeding well.

After Don thumped himself on the noggin with the butt end of his axe head, he soon staggered to his feet and turned his attention to yet another living maple, this one a mere sapling. On this diminutive twig, his axe found purchase. Soon, he had harvested a bundle of twigs and placed them in a tangled heap in the middle of the fire pit. But, how to light them? Igniting green wood is tough enough; igniting wet green wood is nearly impossible. The enterprising Don doused the branches in a pint of white gas, struck a match, and, at the cost of his eyebrows and forearm hair, successfully kindled a fire that emitted a cloud of wet, green smoke. Returning the axe to its sheath on his belt and swaggering like a gunfighter who had just dropped his arch nemesis, Don returned to the shelter.

Soon, the dense smoke was billowing into the shelter, driving all of its occupants out into the rain, except Mark, who was too dazed to move. Squinting through tears, Don joined his partner at the back of the shelter where the two set about preparing dinner by peeling the plastic wrappers from a half-dozen Slim Jims.

"What do you think?" Don asked, biting off a finger-length portion of his evening entreé.

"About what?"

"About the trail."

"I dunno. What do you think?" asked Mark, still staring into the void.

"Do you think we can make it?"

"Where?" Mark asked, suddenly alert. "To Maine? Are you crazy? After all this?"

"No," Don answered. "Back down to Amicalola Falls."

"Well, if we rest up another day, I think I might be up to it."

And so, two days later, after the supply of Slim Jims was spent and some of the color had returned to Mark's cheeks, the two again took up the blue blazes and retreated to Amicalola Falls, promising to return next year—better equipped, better prepared, better conditioned, in better health—to hike the entire Appalachian Trail.

ADLY, THIS TALE OF WOE IS TRUE. I MET DON AND Mark on Springer Mountain while I was on the trail in 1987. They will forever epitomize the misadventures that often befall poorly prepared hikers who—eager but clueless—take up the trail.

As it turns out, the odds are against the hundreds of hikers who, each summer, leave Springer aspiring to reach Maine. During most summers, only about 20 percent will achieve their goal. Owing to a welter of possible complications, the others become wasted along the way, many before they even clear the seventy-eight miles to the North Carolina border. For one thing, there is injury. The Appalachian Trail is, in effect, a nearly continuous, five-month endurance event, and, like any athletic pursuit, it poses limitless potential for injury. Rick, a hiker we had met in Georgia, who seemed to have the mental toughness and stamina to make it all the way, made it only as far as Virginia before he took a spill on a stretch of wet, rocky trail and opened a tendon-deep gash in his knee.

Victor wrenched a calf muscle in the Smokies and, after hobbling along and grimacing for a week, made the painful decision to depart the trail in Hot Springs, North Carolina.

There were less predictable obstacles, too, that led hikers to abandon their hopes. Byron, whom we had befriended in Tennessee, made it as far as New Jersey, we heard, before someone stole his pack while he was off in the brush relieving himself. Without a pack or the funds to buy a new one, Byron was forced to end his hike. One day in Shenandoah National Park in Virginia, we discovered a note pinned to a wooden park service sign at a road crossing. The note, addressed to a hiker behind us whom we didn't know, read:

AS FAR AS THE EYE CAN SEE

Dear _____ ,
Your father has died of a heart attack. Call your sister
for details. Please return home immediately.

There were the psychological factors—boredom, loneliness—
which also reduced our ranks. But, more than anything else, it
was poor planning and conditioning and overloaded packs that
led to failure. Springer Mountain served as a magnet for legions
of uninitiated hikers who bumbled into the woods and who,
often just as quickly, bumbled back out. Incredibly, there were
people who had quit their jobs and drained their bank accounts
to hike the trail without ever having read about it or explored
any of its miles. They based their expectations on their own
romantic visions or secondhand information gleaned from friends
and acquaintances.

Though I never consciously derived pleasure from the misfor-
tunes of others, I confess that I did find solace in their often ridiculous, sometimes humorous, misadventures. During my most
difficult days, in fact, no matter how unfit I felt for life on the trail,
I found that reflecting on some of the unforgivable gaffes of my
colleagues could leave me feeling like Daniel Boone.

We met many of them face to face on the trail, and we read
the accounts of others in shelter registers. More often, we learned
about their desperate straits by the gear they had left behind. All
through Georgia, for instance, shelters were cluttered with heaps
of discarded items: axes, shovels, survival knives, shoes, boots,
socks, shirts, pants, underwear, bras, rain ponchos, canned goods,
cook pots, gallon cans of white gas, plant books, first-aid books,
Bibles (full-sized leather-bound editions), books of poetry, novels,
bird books, insect books, cookbooks.

Often the items were accompanied by notes that, with some
variation, expressed this sentiment:

I am miserable. My pack is too heavy. My feet hurt.
I've decided to cut weight by leaving behind this
garden spade, cast-iron skillet, twelve-inch survival

knife, and two-pound tin of Dinty Moore beef stew. I have not had the opportunity to use them but hope they'll be of service to someone. Heading north. Hoping things improve.

A hardliner would call such disposal of goods littering. Most of the items became permanent fixtures in the shelters. After all, what reasonable hiker seeks to increase his load once he's entered the woods? But then, who condemned the pioneers who lightened their loads by heaving their heirlooms and other expendable items overboard in hopes of successfully crossing the prairies?

We learned that there were other means of lightening one's load. One hiker Dan and I encountered less than one mile below Springer had kindled a trailside fire, which he stoked with heavy volumes on first aid, edible wild plants, birds, and bugs. We stood by, watching him feed the flames. Like a backcountry merchant, he had set out his store of canned goods in orderly stacks, inviting passersby to take whatever they wanted. As if he hadn't suffered enough already under the weight of his pack, he tore the seat out of his trousers when he squatted to extract more extraneous items from his pack.

Then there were the two women I met as I neared the summit of Springer on a later trip. It was raining, and, as I glanced ahead, I spotted the two of them shuffling along as if their legs were bound. In a sense, they were. It seems that one of the women, a seamstress, had crafted "front" packs to supplement the storage capacity of their fully loaded backpacks. The packs, which fastened around the waist, had never been field-tested, and, after a few miles on the trail, they had slipped down, settling around the women's upper thighs and reducing their strides to a series of baby steps.

But, the women had other problems, too. Once in camp, I watched as each woman withdrew from her pack an entire spice rack, crafted from twelve-inch strips of Styrofoam and equipped with twelve or fifteen plastic bottles. Then came the stoves: propane torches and foot-tall iron tripods borrowed from a chemistry lab where one of the women worked. These were not modest propane burners, but heavy foot-long tanks with brass nozzles. The stoves were designed, not to heat metal pots, but to melt them. The cooking outfits also included a metal support for the torches, which directed the blue blade of flame through the ring of the beaker stand and onto the base of the cook pot. After twenty miles of abject misery, the women veered off the trail at the first cross-roads, which led into Suches, Georgia.

Once in town, they dumped the front packs and torches before buying more suitable gear and continuing on.

Then, there were the two fellows from Atlanta who had set out under the mistaken assumption, that once on the trail, there was no means for egress or acquiring supplies. Their determina-tion—and knees—gave out after twenty miles, and they, too, bailed out in Suches.

There was the sweet, naive woman from New York. Plump and in her early twenties, she had set out on the trail by her parents' choosing, not by her own. Her parents had hoped to help their daughter boost her self-confidence and drop a few pounds in the process, and they decided that a 2,100-mile hike along the Ap-palachian Trail might do the trick. So, they bought her a pack, a pair of boots, and a bus ticket to Georgia.

Her first days on the trail were torturous, and it was remarkable that she made it as far as she did. Had it not been for Byron, who found her blubbering in the weeds on the trail in the Smokies, she might still be stranded there. Byron hefted her pack, along with his own, and led her, sobbing, to the next shelter. Once there, Byron assumed the role of big brother and urged her to bail out. She heeded his advice, sort of.

Over the next several weeks, she evolved from an Appalachian Trail hiker to an Appalachian Trail groupie. Frequently, we arrived in trail towns—through most of Georgia, North Carolina, Ten-nessee, and even into Virginia—only to find the woman waiting for us there. She had given up hiking, but not hitchhiking, and, as we would pick up the trail out of town, she would hang her thumb for a lift into the next stop. Bryon repeatedly urged her to go home, fearing that some deranged motorist might take advantage of her, and he went so far as to buy her a bus ticket home, but she persisted. Eventually, she became the basis for a series of bets among hikers: Would she or wouldn't she be waiting for us in the next town?

After Byron had purchased the bus ticket and extracted a promise from her that she would use it, he was so confident that he bet a group of us a milk shake each that, when we arrived in Damascus, Virginia, she would be gone. When we entered town, we spotted her waving from a hotel and hoofed it directly to the local Dairy Queen to collect on our bet.

 HERE THERE ARE SHEEP, THERE ARE ALSO WOLVES, and on the trail, where there are such poorly adapted hikers as the young woman from New York, there are predators out to take unfair advantage of them. The trail's reigning flimflam artist was a man known variously as Mack, Mountain Man Mack, and Ranger Mack. A portly indigent man in his early twenties who hailed from some backwoods settlement, Mack had developed an ingenious scam.

Clad in a forest-service green uniform and wearing a pack, Mack would arrive on the trail in late April as the fresh corps of thru-hikers set out from Springer. He presented himself as an agent of the Forest Service, and he carried a bogus badge and a small side arm. He explained that his mission was to serve as guide to hikers on the Appalachian Trail. Mack boasted that he had hiked the trail end to end, that he knew virtually every edible plant, and that he could steer a hiker safely through even the most formidable disasters. Having won the hikers' confidence, he would then amble along with them, gauging their gullibility as he inventoried their stores of cash and food.

To hikers ill-suited for the rigors of life on the trail and needing guidance, Mack was a godsend, or so he seemed. In exchange for a few dollars a day and a share of their food, he would shepherd

AS FAR AS THE EYE CAN SEE

them through the woods. Slowly. He stolidly refused to walk in the rain, and, even on sunny days, he seldom covered more than five or six miles.

Dan and I met Mack at Rocky Knob Shelter in Georgia the day after a tornado had ripped through the woods a few miles from our camp in Tesnatee Gap. Peering inside the shelter, we spotted Mack with four other hikers. Among them were the woman from New York and a bizarre, bearded man from Maine who seemed to be daft. Both posed perfect targets for Mack. They, along with the other two, had signed on with the shyster, who now sat fat and happy in the shelter eating their food. Why they never became suspicious of him or his alleged background I can't imagine. If he were an official of the Forest Service, why did he require food? If he refused to walk in the rain, how had he completed the trail? And, if he had completed the trail and continued to spend his days hiking, why was he so fat?

We learned later that, one morning near the edge of the Smokies, the hikers had awakened to find themselves alone in the shelter. Having bilked them out of money and food, Mack had vanished. It seems he had an aversion to the Smokies, and later in Hot Springs we would learn why.

A few days after we arrived in Hot Springs, Elmer, the owner of the Inn, explained that Mack, who lived off the kindness— or ignorance—of hapless hikers, was as much a part of spring in the southern Appalachians as the budding flowers. Years earlier, he had been arrested for impersonating a government law-enforcement official and for carrying a concealed weapon without a permit. Even now, Elmer explained, there was a warrant out for his arrest. It seems that, while Mack felt comfortable working his scheme along the little-traveled trails of the national forests, he feared the trails of the national parks, which were populated with armed, *bona fide* rangers.

Elmer was right. Later, while on an early-spring hike with a friend near Hot Springs in 1986, I arrived at Deer Park Mountain Shelter four miles south of town. We sat eating lunch when a shirtless hiker approached from the south, his gut flopping over the hip belt of his pack. He wore stereo headphones connected to a Walkman.

"Been damned hungry the past few days," he said, scratching his protruding belly after shedding his pack. "I hain't had a decent meal for the last four days, and I'm damned near starvin'." He flashed us a toothless grin as he eyed the bag of trail mix that lay on my lap. I offered him a handful, and, when I did, he snatched up the entire bag. Then, his glance moved to the plastic bottle of whiskey beside me.

"That wouldn't be sippin' whiskey would it?" he asked. Though irked by his shameless mooching, I handed him the bottle. Then, he spotted the tin of snuff in my shirt pocket. "And, might I trouble you for a dip?" he continued. "Hain't had a dip for nigh on a week." Again, I obliged.

"God, I'm hungry," he continued.

"You know there's food in town," I suggested. "The Inn has some of the best meals on the whole trail."

"I hain't sure I can make it that far, I'm so darned weak, and my stomach's so empty it hurts," he continued, patting his healthy roll of flab. "And, I hain't got no money A couple guys robbed me back at the last shelter."

It had been years since I had last seen Mack, and, though I didn't immediately recognize the face, his *modus operandi* was unmistakable. I decided to confront him.

"Your name wouldn't be Mack, by any chance?" I asked. An alarmed look spread over his face.

"Well, ah, some people call me that."

"Mountain Man Mack?"

"Well, yeah."

"Ranger Mack?"

"Uh-huh."

I started laughing. In seven years, the trail hadn't changed one bit. The spring was just as beautiful—and Mack just as corrupt—as ever. The reason he was so reluctant to push on into Hot Springs, I surmised, was that he was known there by too many people, people who were wise to his game and might have turned him in to the authorities. He realized he would fare better, and eat better, if he stuck to the trail and plied hikers for food.

"Well, I think it's time to be moseying. Mack, I hope you get some grub," I said, as I piled my gear back into my pack, stood, and climbed into the straps. My friend, who threw me a baffled glance, did the same. As we left the shelter, Mack tried one last ploy to separate me from my cash: "Hey I'll sell you this Walkman for ten dollars." I ignored the offer and, still laughing, kept on walking. Over the few miles to our camp, I explained to my friend that he had met one of the trail's most notorious con men.

Initially, I viewed Mack—and others like him—as a scourge of the trail, but, in time, I've come to regard him in a kinder light. In many ways, he was the same as the mice, chipmunks, raccoons, skunks, feral dogs, and other opportunistic critters who lingered around the shelters and grew fat on our mistakes. But, he was different from his four-legged counterparts in one regard: Once I was on to his tricks, he seemed a lot less clever.

CHAPTER EIGHT

Gear

I never imagined that existence could he so simple, so uncluttered, so Spartan, so free of baggage, so sublimely gratifying. I have reduced the weight of my pack to thirty-five pounds, and yet I can't think of a single thing I really need that I can't find either within myself or within my pack. The pack contains all essentials, as well as a few luxury items: a book, a Frisbee, a quarter-pint of whiskey, and a poem I photocopied at a library a few miles back. Today as I walked, I memorized the poem, "She Walks in Beauty" by Lord Byron, and tonight I will use the paper to kindle a fire and thereby reduce my weight by another ounce.

SEPTEMBER 9, 1979
POPLAR RIDGE LEAN-TO, MAINE

 LIVE ALONE IN A THREE-ROOM CABIN ON THE CUMBERLAND Plateau in east Tennessee. My collected possessions sprawl, clutter, choke. I open closets and confront boxes whose contents remain a complete mystery. I open drawers, searching for pencils or scissors, and sift through a chaos of knickknacks. On the screened porch,

I forage for tools through a tangle of gadgets the functions of which I have long ago forgotten.

Returning from the porch, I spot my former dwelling hanging on a nail. A green nylon frame backpack with a capacity of 2,500 cubic inches. It features one large main compartment, a front pouch, and four side pouches. The largest pouch—in the front—measures nine inches across, seven inches from top to bottom, and two inches deep. Below the pack bag is a vacant section of frame for my sleeping bag.

In 1979, that pack was more than ample to contain the sum total of my worldly possessions—thirty-five to forty-five pounds worth. It included everything—absolutely everything—I really needed:

Two cotton T-shirts, two cotton bandannas, one pair of nylon running shorts, a pair of cotton Army fatigue trousers, one wool shirt, a pair of wool gloves, a coated-nylon rain jacket, two pairs of wool socks, two pairs of thin liner socks, one pair of lug-soled boots for the trail, and a pair of running shoes for camp, a stove and one-liter fuel bottle, a two-quart cook pot, a nylon foodbag, one plastic film canister filled with salt and another filled with pepper, a steel drinking cup, one metal spoon with bent handle, two one-liter plastic water bottles, a six-ounce plastic bottle for distilled spirits, one bottle of water-purification tablets, a toothbrush and small tube of toothpaste, a three-ounce bottle of biodegradable soap, a fifty-foot length of parachute cord for hanging food, a synthetic-fill sleeping bag rated to thirty-five degrees, a closed-cell foam sleeping mat, a first-aid kit, a trail guidebook, a paperback book, a spiral-bound notebook in which I recorded my journal, a billed cap, insect repellent, a rainfly, a Swiss Army knife, a butane lighter, and a partial roll of toilet paper.

How would I begin, I wonder, to prioritize what I own today and select thirty-five pounds from all this tonnage, thirty-five pounds that would answer my needs and leave me feeling as secure and well outfitted as I felt in 1979? I suspect I couldn't. Even if I were to fill my pack with the same items, I realize I could not resurrect the sense of self-sufficiency. Or the freedom that came from knowing that, wherever I found myself at noonday or night-fall, my house and its goods rested beside me.

No. The years away from the trail have softened me, made me reliant on creature comforts. Certainly, I can and do release my hold on them when I return to the trail for a few days or even a week, but for five months? I would feel naked, vulnerable. I would, in spite of myself, imagine a host of dire what-if contingencies requiring the addition of first one item, then another and another until my pack strained at its seams and refused to accommodate any more.

At one time, my pack was an extension of myself. It accompanied me everywhere I went. When I carried it, it rode on my back as naturally as a flesh-and-bone appendage. And even after I took it off, my hands probed its pockets and hidden folds as precisely as I might have reached to scratch an unseen itch. I could locate any item, no matter how small or deeply buried, as quickly and surely as I might have raised a finger to touch my nose or flick an insect from my ear. I was like a snail or turtle whose den is a fixed companion along all the miles of its life.

Someone on the trail once shared with me a simple principle for reducing my pack to the bare essentials. "If you don't use an item at least once a day," he said, "get rid of it."

It was sound advice. With the exception of the items in my first-aid kit, some of which I never used, I abided by that principle. In the interest of economy, like most hikers, I devised methods for extending the utility of the items I did carry.

My sleeping bag, for instance, fulfilled its primary task of insulating my body from the elements. It served almost as efficiently as a refrigerator. A quart of ice cream nestled at the core of a sleeping bag in its stuff sack would survive summertime heat and provide a refreshing dessert hours and miles out of town. My closed-cell foam pad served equally well as a beer or soda cooler or as a comfortable sleeping mat. I could roll three chilled cans tightly in the eight-foot-long pad, stopper the ends with wool socks, and enjoy a cold beer with dinner six or eight hours later.

And, when laid against a tree trunk, the pad served as a chaise longue for afternoon naps.

The plumber's candles I carried were effective fire starters, and when set on an overturned drinking cup, they provided ample light for reading or writing after dark. The flexible round screen—made from heavy-gauge aluminum foil—that circled my stove and shielded it from the wind doubled as a lantern reflector. If I folded it in half, bent it into an arc, and then placed it behind a candle, it would illuminate an entire shelter. The windscreen also served as a spout if laid amid the rocks in a slow-moving spring that trickled down a hillside.

The fifty feet of nylon parachute cord I carried served several functions. Evenings, I tied a stone to one end, hurled it over a sturdy branch, secured the end to our nylon food bags, and hoisted it out of reach of raccoons and bears. The line served equally well as a clothesline, and I found that, if I doubled the cord and twisted it before securing it to two trees, I could hang my socks, bandanna, shirt, and shorts by threading the fabric between the twisted filaments. Even the stiffest breeze could not pluck them free. And once, when my pack bag tore from one of its grommets, I used the cord to secure the bag to the frame.

The needle and packet of dental floss I carried in my first-aid kit provided sturdy, waxed-nylon thread for repairing packs, clothes, and boots. My metal drinking cup held my evening tea, but it also served as a bowl for my morning oatmeal and a scoop for drawing water from pools too shallow to accept a water bottle or cook pot. My Frisbee provided postdinner diversion and served as a fine plate.

Once filled, my two-and-a-half-gallon waterbag, a plastic pouch housed in a purple nylon sack and outfitted with a rubber nozzle, contained ample water for evening meals and drinks. Once emptied of water and inflated with air, it made a comfortable pillow.

My two one-liter water bottles doubled as rehydrating containers, and a handful of dried beans or lentils dropped into a bottle of water in the morning would be swollen and ready to cook by the time I arrived in camp in the afternoon.

The rain fly I carried provided emergency shelter and doubled as a groundsheet, protecting my sleeping bag from damp earth. The coated nylon anorak, a light jacket I carried, repelled rain, and, in cool weather, I layered it over my wool shirt to retain body heat.

The three-and-one-half-ounce tuna tins I carried as my primary source of protein served, when empty, to thwart the critters who attempted to pillage our food bags at night. I baked the empty tin in the fire to remove the odor and then poked a hole in the can's bottom with my knife. Then I tied a knot halfway down the line from my foodbag and threaded the cord through the hole before I hung the bag. The upside-down can, situated midway on the hanging line, presented an impasse for the craftiest of mice.

Even my wool gloves served a dual purpose. They warmed my hands on chill, wet days, and they acted as hot pads for plucking boiling pots from the coals. Hikers caught by cold temperatures without gloves found that wool socks doubled as warm mittens.

If the contents of our packs couldn't answer our needs, we turned to the forest for aid. Our ingenuity, combined with the raw resources of the wilderness, resolved most problems.

Stiff rhododendron leaves or short sticks split in half and cleaned of their center core provided spouts when inserted into slow-trickling springs. When downed deadwood was drenched by rains, we could always find dry kindling by shaking the trunks of standing dead trees. The trunks telegraphed and amplified the swaying motion to the tops of the trees, which whipped furiously and cracked, releasing a hail of dead branches. Because of their vertical orientation, those top branches escaped the brunt of drenching rains and dried quickly in the air circulating through the treetops.

When our cook pots became crusted with baked-on food, we used nature's scouring pad, a handful of sand and pebbles from a stream bed. A cook pot laid in a stream and anchored with a stone on its lid would cool instant pudding, and forked sticks driven into the ground near the fire and spanned with a wooden crossbar would provide a perfect drying rack for wet socks and clothing. We used the same spits for dangling pots over the flames. Flat rocks served as cutting boards for chopping vegetables and as dining tables.

 F WE WEREN'T TURNING TO THE WILDERNESS FOR solutions, we turned to it for amusement. Through the five months I spent on the trail, I do not recall ever once being bored for want of something to occupy my time in camp. There was always something to do or see.

Just before we reached the Lake Country in Maine, for instance, I had my parents send me my telescoping fishing rod, and I spent evenings angling for supplemental protein and for fun. The rod provided dinner for a half-dozen hikers when we reached Antlers Camp, an abandoned fishing camp on the shores of a pristine backwoods lake fifty miles south of Mount Katahdin. Situated on a rocky peninsula, the camp contained a series of old log cabins, the main cabin featuring a wood-burning stove and an iron skillet; it was perfect for a fish-fry. After arriving in the early afternoon, I pulled on my wool shirt, grabbed my fishing rod, and followed the curve of the shoreline three-quarters of a mile from camp. Perched on a rock and surrounded by flaming sugar maples and golden birches, I reeled in a dozen lake trout. Two hours later, when I arrived back in camp, I discovered that Dan, Paul, and two other hikers who shared our camp had spent the afternoon harvesting freshwater clams from the rocky shore.

That evening, Dan played chef, frying our fillets and mussels in butter, and we took our evening meal on the shoreline in front of a fire. As we ate, we watched the red sash of sunset ripple on the wind-buffeted surface of the lake.

Then, there was stargazing, a diversion I could never get enough of. There were always mysterious specks—satellites, probably—floating in the seas of the heavens, which invariably led to discussion regarding life on other planets or extraterrestrials. And meteors. We would lie on our backs in open fields under the canopy of a real-life planetarium and fix on the star-flecked heavens. Although we had witnessed dozens of meteor showers, we could never contain the *ooohs* and *ahhs* that escaped as the bright objects arced across black skies, spilling trails of golden glitter.

Bird-watching became another favorite pastime. I once sat at the base of a hardwood tree in Maine watching a pileated woodpecker probe the bark for grubs directly above me while his manic excavation showered me with wood chips.

And night hikes. As fearful as I had been in my first days in Georgia of the dark woods and mysterious night sounds, I later found in the dark woods a sanctuary where I could sit alone and think in the company of the animals. I often strayed away from camp, following the beam of my flashlight until I found a comfortable roost on a rock or fallen log. Then, I switched off the flashlight and instantly was enveloped in the womb of darkness. Without my sense of sight, my hearing and touch became heightened, and I could follow the progress of large and small creatures as they moved around and past me. Chipmunks, skunks, mice, and squirrels scurried, while deer cracked and thudded. As deer approached, I could hear the branches snap and feel the ground vibrating under the heavy impact of their hooves.

But the night woods weren't always serene. One night in Connecticut, I left camp and found a seat in a grove of hemlock along the Housatonic River. It was perfectly still when a hoot owl perched in the tree behind me suddenly unleashed its eerie call. From a distance of twenty feet, it boomed as if through an amplified speaker. Spooked, I started and jumped to my feet. Equally startled, the owl took flight, and I heard its wing tips slap the hemlock branches as it retreated.

Streams were favorite spots for evening reveries. They titillated the ears and the eyes. If we listened, we could hear the lapping water trace the entire musical scale in a random melody of ethereal notes and chords, and, if we probed the water with our flashlight beams, we could watch scads of bizarre performers—nymphs, water spiders, crayfish, minnows—as they ducked and darted, scampered and scuttled in and out of the spotlight.

There were times, too, when we used the streams as aquatic sports arenas. In mid-May, for instance, Dan and I camped near a stream in the Devils Creek watershed in Tennessee, where we staged the Devils Creek Regatta. We used our pocket knives to carve small boats from dead wood. Rocks wedged into the boats' undersides provided ballast, and we even went so far as to gouge holes for masts. We established a starting line at the head of a thirty-yard stretch of flat water; a chute where the water narrowed to a falls marked the finish line. For two hours, until darkness made it impossible to follow the course of the boats, we ran the river, and, before it was over, each of us skippered a fleet of six or eight boats, some built for speed, some built for stability, and others built for the beauty of their intricate hulls.

There were other games, too. In Maine, after we had resupplied in Caratunk, we left town and covered thirteen miles before deciding to hole up in an abandoned barn near a road crossing. After we sat idle for half an hour, Nick discovered a length of wire, which he soon wound into four rings. We drove sharpened stakes into the ground, twenty yards apart, and engaged in game after game of Appalachian Trail horseshoes.

My favorite pastime, though, was reading. Along the trail, I read a dozen books, mainly on nature or the environment. Among them were Thoreau's *Walden*, Annie Dillard's *Pilgrim at Tinker Creek*, and Whitman's *Leaves of Grass*.

I had read Whitman and Thoreau in high school, but, in the classroom of the Appalachian wilderness, their writing came to life. I could peer up from any page and find living examples of the words.

I recall reading a passage from Walden while I was camped in the Lake Country of Maine less than one hundred miles from Katahdin. We were literally following in Thoreau's footsteps, he having visited the area in 1846. Though we explored those mountains 133 years later, the words were written about me, about us, about our carefree existence, and about anyone who seeks communion with the wilderness:

Remember thy creator in the days of thy youth. Rise free from care before the dawn, and seek adventures. Let the noon find thee by other lakes, and the night overtake thee everywhere at home. There are no larger fields than these, no worthier games than here may be played. Grow wild according to thy nature, like these sedges and brakes.

Let the thunder rumble; what if it threaten ruin to farmers' crops? That is not its errand to thee. Take shelter under the cloud, while they flee to carts and sheds. Let not to get a living be thy trade, but thy sport. Enjoy the land, but own it not. Through want of enterprise and faith, men are where they are, buying and selling, and spending their lives like serfs.

CHAPTER NINE

Stopping Along the Way

Last night in Port Clinton, Pennsylvania, Dan and I learned once again that the magic of comradeship does not end at the trailhead but often extends into the small towns along the route. We spent the evening at the Port Clinton Hotel bar in the small blue-collar town with Chuck the snake handler, the boom-pa lady, and a handful of other colorful personalities, and we departed town this morning with a new page of names in our address books.

Those hikers who blast in and out of town, stopping only long enough to fill their stomachs and their foodbags, are missing a vital part of the trail experience. But, even though I've been on the trail for months and have on many occasions been greeted with warmth and acceptance by total strangers, I still occasionally struggle with feelings of mistrust. I'm left wondering why someone would open himself to me when all he stands to gain in return is my own trust and acceptance. Such feelings, I suspect, result from lessons we're taught from the time we're very young. I wonder if they'll survive beyond completion of my hike.

JULY 21, 1979
ALLENTOWN HIKING CLUB SHELTER, PENNSYLVANIA

PRIL 24 INTRODUCED ME TO NEW EXTREMES OF experience. The previous night we had weathered a fierce thunderstorm that left the woods strewn with splintered branches and uprooted trees. The following day wasn't much better. After leaving camp, we trudged through cold rain and ankle-deep muck, and, over the long afternoon, my thoughts turned again and again to the comforts of town.

By early evening, when we finally slipped down an embankment and landed on paved Georgia Highway 75, we faced a decision: We could continue up the trail through more muck and cold rain, or we could follow the road to more inviting surroundings. Though we had not planned a town stop for another few days, we consulted our maps, hung our thumbs, and set out for Helen, Georgia, a tourist resort of alpine chalets and quaint restaurants nine miles to the south.

After scoring a ride from a sympathetic local in a big car, Dan and I, along with four other sodden hikers, were soon ensconced in a cut-rate motel room—twenty-six dollars a night for the bunch of us—and drawing lots for the shower. En route to the motel, we had cajoled our driver into stopping at a local package store and a pizza joint before he deposited us at the motel office.

Six showers and an hour later, the room lay in shambles. Fetid shirts, shorts, boots, and socks lay in dank, aromatic piles in corners and on counter tops. Pack covers and rain parkas dripped from curtain rods. Pizza boxes and empty beer bottles cluttered bedside tables. In the bathroom, dirt-smudged towels steeped in standing water, and a dark water stain crept along the all-weather carpet from the bathroom into the bedroom. The soil we had rinsed from our bodies formed a miniature delta at the drain in the bathtub.

But, none of us seemed to notice the clutter, or, if we did, we didn't much care. We were too busy indulging our wanton appetites. It wasn't until we switched on the television that it occurred to us that our few days on the trail had already wrought some changes.

We watched a special program about the life of American novelist Thomas Wolfe. The story of Wolfe, a true iconoclast, appealed to our own sense of freewheeling independence. Then, a commercial came on the screen. It was an unremarkable advertisement—for corn chips or glass cleaner or hair spray—but it had an unusual effect. We laughed. We roared. We howled. We cried. Not so much at the product itself but at the realization that the world of fresh-smelling houses, clean-shaven faces, sporty sedans, dutiful housewives, and industrious husbands no longer connected with ours. The commercial clearly had been directed at someone else.

The next morning, we made a quick stop at a local grocery store, hitchhiked back to the trailhead, and again picked up the white blazes. Even though we faced another day of rain and muck, those things seemed much less dismal. Our twelve hours in town had restored us, but the town stop had done more than that. It had provided evidence that, by following the trail, we had strayed into a strange new realm where the attractions of civilization, though still appealing, had assumed a new role, and I realized that, with months remaining ahead of us, this shift in attitude was only the beginning.

ELEN, GEORGIA, WAS OUR FIRST TOWN STOP, AND, over the next several months, we visited dozens of villages, cities, back-road hamlets, and crossroads. As it turned out, those outposts of civilization were in some ways as vital to the trail experience as the mountains themselves.

The towns allowed us to phone friends and relatives to catch up on important news from home. News from home that did not reach us *via* the phone lines usually awaited our arrival at the local post offices, where postal clerks processed and held scores of boxes—boxes of supplies, care packages, and letters—addressed to us in care of general delivery.

Towns afforded us breaks from the routine of big-mile days, and we celebrated the long, steep descents that led us into those settlements, just as working men and women might have welcomed the five-o'clock whistle that marked the onset of a holiday.

Towns also exposed us to the distinctive people and cultures of the various regions of the eastern United States. Along the way, we encountered open, slow-talking Southerners; circumspect residents of the populous mid-Atlantic states; and wry, taciturn New Englanders. Each region and town provided its own brand of succor.

Most important, towns provided needed supplies. Without them, we would have been forced either to carry five months' worth of food on our backs or to subsist on roots and berries. The first option, I suspect, would have left us crippled; the second might have left us dead, owing to our familiarity with only a few edible plants.

Food. Though we cursed it for all the weight a five- or seven-day supply added to the pack on the stiff ascents out of town, we also celebrated it when, during the first days along a new section, the foodbag promised both plenty and variety.

Then, toward the end of that same stretch, when our reserves ran low and we subsisted on the dregs of the food sack, we became obsessed by food, talked about it incessantly, craved it, longed for it. Mountains of ice cream, bags of cookies, slabs of red meat, bowls of crisp greens, and boxes of pastries, cakes, and pies—those were the stuff of hikers' dreams during the last few days and nights before a resupply stop.

Consider that most long-distance hikers eat and metabolize as many as six thousand calories a day. After the first couple of weeks on the trail, when exertion tends initially to suppress a hiker's appetite, most end-to-enders succumb to an incurable case of "hiker's disease," an affliction characterized by an appetite that simply cannot be satisfied.

I could not count the number of times I confronted stunned expressions on onlookers' faces as they observed my colleagues and me wandering along the aisles of a food market dazed and bewitched by the abundance while trying to decide what to consume first, second, third. . . . We were, in effect, prisoners of want suddenly freed in a climate-controlled environment of excess, and, in weaker moments, my companions and I were likely to consume half-gallons of ice cream, pound bags of cookies, and quarts of fruit juice before returning to the store for the second course.

Our binge eating wasn't limited to grocery stores. In Elk Park, North Carolina, for instance, three other hikers and I arrived at a restaurant soon after it opened on a Sunday afternoon, paid our three dollars each, and consumed the entire contents of a salad bar before the owner politely but firmly invited us to move on.

In a northern Virginia town, I spent five hours at an all-you-can-eat restaurant with another hiker, downing dozens of plates of steamed shrimp. We finally left the establishment more to ease the finger cramps that resulted from peeling so much shellfish than because we had eaten our fill.

The challenge we faced as caloric consumers, as I liked to describe it, was to "toe the fine line between bliss and nausea." Regrettably, I crossed that line on occasion and suffered the consequences. On one such night in Gorham, New Hampshire, after first visiting the local McDonald's, I ate five heaping bowls of a vegetable stew we had prepared in the kitchen of the Congregational church where we were permitted to stay. When I had choked down the last spoonful, I staggered out onto the church lawn, unbuttoned my pants to relieve some of the pressure on my bloated abdomen, and lay in the grass, moaning like a pregnant mare in the throes of labor. As I did, I prayed for the nausea to pass and vowed never to eat that much again. I kept my resolution only until we arrived in the next town.

NCE WE HAD PURCHASED OUR SUPPLIES AT A MAR-
ket, it was customary for us to sit on the store's
stoop, alternately loading supplies into our packs
and wedging morsels into our mouths. The process
of taking products from the shelves and preparing
them for the backcountry became known as "throwing away
Madison Avenue." Essentially, the process involved stripping off
the boxes, wrappers, bags, and canisters, which catered more to
the strategies of marketing executives than to the needs of backcountry travelers. Once we had removed the items from their
packages, we deposited them in plastic bags. The bags were durable, as well as flexible, and they allowed us to take full advantage
of every available square inch of pack space. Eliminating Madison
Avenue also spared us several pounds of useless heft.

Though at times it seemed that we hikers took more than we
gave in each of those towns, filling our stomachs and food bags
before moving on, I like to think that an equitable exchange took
place when hikers visited civilization. Because many of the trail
towns lay far off the main roads, townsfolk often embraced us as
ambassadors of good will and seemed never to tire of our tales of
adventure from the surrounding woods.

Local merchants welcomed our business, and they stocked
their shelves with dietary staples—macaroni-and-cheese, pasta
noodles, rice, peanut butter, English muffins, lentils, summer
sausage, instant oatmeal, sardines, granola bars, honey—that
were perfectly suited to our transient needs. Innkeepers often
allowed us to pile as many as ten hikers into a room designed to
accommodate two, and they often adjusted their rates to ease
the jolt to our meager budgets.

Most townsfolk were accustomed to having legions of straggly
foot travelers loose in their streets, and they afforded us all the
courtesy of temporary residents. We brought curious stares from
tourists unfamiliar with the trail, and they often seemed puzzled
and fascinated by our peculiar avocation. Their questions seldom
varied: Where do you sleep? What do you do when it rains? What
do you eat? Seen any snakes? Seen any bears? Don't your feet hurt?

Where did you start? Where are you headin'? Why are you doing this? Our responses soon became as pat and predictable as the questions themselves, but I, for one, enjoyed sharing my experiences with anyone interested enough to listen.

Along our journey, we logged a series of fond memories of our stopovers, some because of novelty, others because of kindness shown us. A few were because of the rich relationships we enjoyed with our hosts.

At Wesser, North Carolina, a settlement set on the banks of the Nantahala River, 137 miles north of Springer, we sat for hours in the rustic health-food restaurant eating fresh-baked herb bread and peering through picture windows at kayakers navigating the rapids below. In Damascus, Virginia, known as the friendliest town on the trail, we lodged in a two-story hostel dubbed The Place, which was owned and operated by the Methodist church. We spent the evening swapping tales with our brothers and sisters on two wheels—transcontinental cyclists—who had embarked on the Centennial Route that passed through town and continued on to the West Coast.

In Charlottesville, Virginia, Dan and I crashed in a dilapidated fraternity house with walls and doors pocked with fist- and head-sized holes, and we spent the evening in a local pub listening to live country music.

In Duncannon, Pennsylvania, on the Susquehanna River, we shared the basement of the city firehouse with a foursome of teachers who worked with mentally disabled children.

Dan and I arrived in Port Clinton, Pennsylvania, on a Saturday afternoon and found our way to a covered pavilion that the city had designated as an overnight area for hikers. By dusk, after cranking a hand pump and washing the grit from my face, arms, and legs, I wandered through the streets of the working-class town. The place looked drab and depressed, and, had it not been for the experiences that awaited me, I would have forever viewed Port Clinton as a decaying, lifeless burg on the verge of economic ruin.

On the way back to the pavilion, I wandered into the lounge

at the Port Clinton Hotel and took a seat at the bar. Once inside, I suspected I had strayed into another establishment of the Erwin, Tennessee, ilk. The working-class locals perched on bar stools studied me closely, but none acknowledged me directly. I ordered a beer, which cost me twenty-five cents, and as I sipped it, I noticed that the bartender had deposited a handful of small plastic tokens in front of me. I finished the beer and ordered another, but, when I tried to pay for it, the bartender motioned toward the tokens. "Son, the rest of your beers have already been paid for."

These stone-faced locals, it seems, were not as dour as they looked. Once I realized that I sat surrounded by benefactors, I hefted my mug and toasted them. Whatever doubts I had had about the character of those folks vanished with my next draught, and, in minutes, I sat surrounded by local men and women, all hungry for news from the trail.

After a half-hour of chatter about the trail, a woman in her mid-thirties entered the room carrying a curious contraption that resembled a pogo stick adorned with cymbals, bells, a tambourine, a snare drum, and a squeeze horn. She greeted me, walked over to the juke box, and dropped a nickel into the slot. Soon, Bobby Vinton's voice crooned the "Beer Barrel Polka" through the speakers. She then began lurching around the dance floor, bouncing the contraption, which unleashed a cacophonous din of clangs and crashes in time with the music. After a brief demonstration, she handed the device to me.

"This is called a 'boom-pa,'" she said. "And, it's customary for the guest of honor to play it on the first song."

I was both honored and mortified. By now, the bar had attracted a standing-room-only crowd, and all eyes were turned on me. Again, she selected the Bobby Vinton tune on the juke box, and I tentatively stepped to the center of the dance floor and, laughing, began pounding and clanging with as much enthusiasm as I could muster. The bar's patrons soon encircled me, raising their beer mugs and cheering me on. When the tune ended, I returned to my seat to a round of applause. I had been duly initiated.

The boom-pa's clamorous din and the crowd noise had apparently carried several city blocks to the pavilion and reached Dan's ears. Drawn by his curiosity, he followed the sound to the bar, and, when he passed through the door, I announced to my newfound friends that it would only be fitting to afford Dan the same honor they had extended to me. Soon the polka tune roared through the speakers, and I sat back and laughed as Dan plied the boom-pa and received the same frenzied response.

Normally cool and composed, Dan sat with his mouth agape for some minutes after his boom-pa debut, and I felt obliged to explain our good fortune. As I explained the bargain beers, at twenty-five cents a draught, and the juke box, where a quarter bought five plays, he, too, began to amass the small tokens. Before long, both of us were gloriously drunk, sitting at the bar and hobnobbing with the other patrons as intimately as if we had shared the same parentage. Among them was a toothless fellow named Chuck, a self-described snake charmer who claimed to keep rattlers in his car as insurance against thieves. Though Dan and I were accustomed to providing tales of wild adventure, we yielded to a more masterful storyteller and passed the evening hours listening to Chuck relate fascinating—though unlikely—Indian legends, mountain ghost tales, and sorcery yarns.

When Dan and I departed Port Clinton the next morning, the town appeared much more vibrant and alive than it had when we arrived.

Several weeks later, we again encountered good fortune near Unionville, New York, at the lakeside home of Gary, a New Age minister, and his wife and two sons. Dan and I—along with Paul, who had since joined our group—had met Gary at a road crossing a week south of Unionville when he stopped to give us a lift to the local grocery store. Back at the trailhead, he gave us his phone number and invited us to call him when we reached Unionville.

A few days later, we phoned him from the trailhead, piled into the back of his car, and soon arrived at his house. That evening, after we had enjoyed a lavish gourmet feast on the lakeside deck,

Gary, an accomplished musician, uncorked a bottle of wine, lighted a candelabra, and serenaded us with beautiful classical music on his baby grand piano. It was the first music we had heard for weeks, and Paul and Dan, both musicians themselves, sat rapt through Gary's performance.

The next day, we accompanied Gary and his wife to a formal lawn party. The host and his family occupied a massive country estate with manicured grounds and a private tennis court. A live rock band performed in a covered gazebo. Most of the few dozen guests sported designer-label togs. Dressed in our cutoff fatigue pants, rag wool socks, and tattered shirts, we looked like a trio of vagabonds who had strayed away from the local mission, but we soon discovered that our shabby dress, and our status as Appalachian Trail thru-hikers, only enhanced our romantic mystique among the hippie-turned-yuppie partygoers.

Paul and I borrowed a couple of rackets and spent the afternoon on the tennis courts. Between sets, we raided the twenty-foot banquet table heaped with enough food to pitch a famished hiker into delirium. There were steamed clams and crabs, roast beef, ham, deviled eggs, salads, fresh fruit, fresh-baked bread, and kegs of iced beer.

After a two-day stay with Gary, we returned to the trail. Over the next several weeks, we frequently found packages filled with books, food, and tidings waiting for us at post offices, courtesy of our zany friend.

Farther north, we splashed in a lake with children from Pawling, New York. While in Pawling, on a dare, I had my ear pierced. In Hanover, New Hampshire, we dined on five-star dormitory fare in Thayer Hall at Dartmouth—one of the more expensive colleges in the United States—and stayed at a former fraternity house that then housed both men and women and where the term "coed" applied even to the showers and the bathrooms.

Our passage through New Hampshire's White Mountains—the most punishing section of the trail—was fortified in part by a visit by Paul's mother, who lived in nearby Peterborough. When our gang—Nick, Dan, Paul, and Victor, the friend who had left the trail in North Carolina—reached Franconia Notch northeast of North Woodstock, New Hampshire, we thumbed the few miles to a park at Profile Lake and met Mrs. Dillon, a jovial woman in her mid-forties. She had arrived in a station wagon brimming with things that trail life had deprived us of: a guitar, cold beer, and food. As we shuttled the food from the car, Mrs. Dillon confessed that she had been cooking for the better part of a week, and it showed. There were pans of fried chicken, plates of deviled eggs, a half-dozen cakes, cookies, and salads: potato salad, tossed salad, macaroni salad, Jell-O salad, cole slaw, fruit salad.

Throughout the long, sun-drenched afternoon, we sidled up to the picnic table, ate our fill, and rolled into the grass, only to begin the cycle again an hour later. Despite our efforts to find the bottoms of all the bowls, plates, and pans, there seemed to be no end to the food, and, when we said good-bye to Mrs. Dillon, we loaded all the surplus we could carry into our packs and happily strained up the trail as if we had shouldered a load of gold bricks.

In Rangeley, Maine, the town of dowdy vacationing retirees, a snooty teller in a posh tourist's bank glanced at my shabby clothes, refused to cash a one-hundred-dollar postal money order, and told me that no one should visit Rangeley without sufficient cash. A few blocks up the street, the teller at an austere, prefab working-man's bank cashed my check without a blink and for a half-hour engaged me in conversation about the trail.

Monson, Maine, is the last outpost of civilization for one hundred miles for hikers headed north, and a church converted to a boarding house provides lodging for most hikers passing through town. For some days prior to reaching Monson, we had heard stories about curious goings-on in the town, which is situated on the fringe of the northern wilderness. There were stories about a haggard alcoholic—a resident at the church—who was prone to pester hikers and plead with them for spare change to feed his habit.

Though many stories grow with each telling as they're passed from hiker to hiker, the word on Monson was, if anything, muted compared with what we discovered when we arrived there.

Once in town, Paul opted to spend the extra money and stay at Shaw's Boarding House, a quaint bed-and-breakfast run by Mr. and Mrs. Shaw, while Dan and I, both watching our budgets, chose to stay at the church.

When I arrived at the church, a square-jawed man in his sixties sat on the stoop. He wore thick glasses, seemed alert and well-mannered, and asked me about the trail. After he helped me find a bunk in the church loft, he ushered me through the converted church while I kept an eye open for the belligerent drunk I had heard so much about.

I didn't realize it at the time, but I had already met him. After about an hour, the man approached me and asked me for seventy-five cents. Still disinclined to believe this was the man who had inspired the rumors, I handed him a dollar. He took it and walked directly to the local package store, where he bought a pint of Old Duke wine. By 2:00 p.m., he had finished his first bottle. Through the afternoon, he systematically begged enough change from other hikers to buy his second, third, and fourth rounds.

By early evening, his eyes were bleary and glazed, his speech was slurred, and he had become the gruff, abrasive character we had been warned about.

"Break my arm, son," he muttered to me, thrusting his stout forearm in my direction. "Ain't no man can break my arm."

I learned later that he was challenging me to arm-wrestle. When I declined, he moved along and challenged other hikers. Soon, one of the other hikers called his bluff and squared off with him over the kitchen table. In spite of the muscular physique he had developed while working as a logger, the drunken man offered little resistance, and the hiker slammed his arm to the table. Tears welled in the old man's eyes, and he stumbled back to his room to the companionship of the Old Duke.

He emerged some time later as Dan and I fixed dinner in the church kitchen. Though he was still drunk, his disposition had softened somewhat, and he sat muttering unintelligibly at the table. As we ate our dinner, he disappeared and returned a few minutes later with a stack of ancient black-and-white photos. "This is my mother," he mumbled, pointing to an attractive woman in turn-of-the-century dress. "This is me," he continued, indicating a much younger, smiling version of himself surrounded by classmates in a grade-school photograph. A later photo showed him—young and strong—in a military uniform, his shoulders straining the seams of his shirt and his stout neck encircled by a tie.

"Then I could break any man's arm," he said, tapping the picture. He curled his arm and pointed to his biceps.

As he continued through the photos, he began to cry. The cry became a moan, and soon he sat alone in a corner of the kitchen, weeping, his eyes closed.

As I sat watching him slump, blubbering, into unconsciousness, I wanted to cry with him. The schoolboy he had pointed out to me in the photo had, no doubt, viewed his future with as much hope and promise as his classmates had. Where had he gotten off track? What had destroyed him?

That evening, I climbed the loft to my bed at 10:30 p.m. and slept soundly for several hours. Then, I heard a sound I'll never forget. It started at 2:00 a.m. from below the rafters and jarred me awake. It was simply the most pitiful sound I've ever heard. It began with the sound of retching, as if the old man were coughing up his heart and lungs. For a half hour, he gagged and vomited, and, when the wave of nausea had passed, the retching was replaced by moaning and wailing. Then, more retching. And more moaning. So it went through the night.

By dawn, he apparently had purged his guts and his emotional reserves, and I found him sitting in the kitchen early the next morning, his eyes clear. He was alert, and the belligerence was gone; he was the same polite, quiet man I had met upon arriving the previous day. He was ready to start a new day to meet new hikers, to ply them for more change, to follow the same worn path to the package store, to run through his dog-eared photographs, and, finally, to pass the night gagging on bile and despair.

Out of town and back on the trail, I found a cluster of young ferns, picked a few sprigs, and rolled them between my palms. I held them to my nose, breathed in the sweet musk, and rejoiced in knowing that one hundred miles lay between me and the next town. As I walked, I wondered for the first time in my life, what it would be like to grow old.

CHAPTER TEN

Hot Springs Rhapsody

We're back on the trail again, after spending ten days in Hot
Springs, North Carolina. I've never been one to abide traditional religious values or to put much stock in spiritual transformation or rebirth, but I know that my stay in Hot Springs
showed me more, taught me more, and changed me more than
any other experience of my life. During our stay, after working
in the fields and talking with Randall and Elmer, I felt as though
I had awakened from a long sleep and for the first time began
to experience the reality of the world around me. I left town
today not only renewed physically but utterly transformed
spiritually. After this, I wonder what other experiences await
me farther north.

MAY 19, 1979
SPRING MOUNTAIN SHELTER, TENNESSEE

IS A GIFT TO BE SIMPLE, 'TIS A GIFT TO BE FREE, 'TIS a gift to end up where you ought to be," Randall sang, giving life to an old Shaker hymn as he scratched the bow across the strings of his fiddle. I joined in the chorus. Dan did, too. The words seemed to capture the essence of what we had experienced since arriving in Hot Springs, North Carolina, a few days earlier.

As I stood at the edge of a furrowed field bristling with newly planted sorghum shoots, I was surrounded by friends: Dan, Randall, the proprietor of the farm, and Elmer, Randall's business partner, who operated a restored Victorian hotel three miles down the serpentine two-lane in town. The hotel, dubbed the Inn, had become a New Age mecca for hikers, where dinner-time brought lavish five-course vegetarian meals and conversation that invariably explored philosophy, religion, and politics. Both Randall and Elmer, as ordained ministers and children of the sixties, were well-versed in all three topics. Elmer had studied at Duke University, Randall at Yale.

Above and around the expanse of cleared farmland, the densely forested peaks of the Pisgah National Forest probed a cloudless, blue, evening sky. Randall, a tall, thin man in his mid-forties with a bushy beard that reached to his chest and shoulder-length hair coiled into a bun at the top of his head, continued his serenade, which he explained was more for the benefit of his crops than for his human audience. Randall's grandpappy, who had lived and died a farmer in these mountains, had told his grandson that fiddling to a newly planted field would ensure a healthy crop.

"'Tis a gift to be simple ... ," Randall continued.

The lyrics of the hymn might have been written about Randall himself and his bohemian lifestyle, and they characterized the wonderful dichotomy he represented. On one hand, he was a man who had traveled the world and had been educated at one of the nation's most prestigious universities. On the other, he was a man born and bred in the nearby mountains, who had returned from his travels with a yen to regain his roots, to embrace the solitude provided by a backcountry farm, to "wind up where he ought to be." In spite of his theological education, or perhaps because of it, he believed in the magic of such simple mountain folkways as fiddling to a field of fledgling crops just as fervently as he believed in the inherent goodness of the Earth. Standing there beneath the mountains and in the company of friends, I began to believe in it, too. Dan and I had spent the preceding five days in Hot Springs, at the Inn and on the farm, and in that time I had discovered that this small North Carolina hamlet was more than just another resupply stop. It was Eden, a place where hikers could find nourishment, love, acceptance, awakening. For me, it provided all those things and more.

Randall and Elmer were two spiritual teachers who had risen out of the ashes of the sixties, preserving all the finest precepts of that era—brotherhood, sharing, love, peace, respect for nature—and carrying the banner into a new age. Because of them, my stay in Hot Springs showed me more, taught me more, and changed me more than any other experience on the trail. When Dan and I resumed our hike after a ten-day rest, I left the town renewed physically and awakened spiritually.

We had arrived in Hot Springs on May 11, tired and haggard from our first three weeks on the trail. Though our blisters had healed, we had encountered the second, and in some ways more debilitating, stage of physical afflictions that plague long-distance hikers. Under the pounding of fifteen- to twenty-mile days, our joints—knees and ankles—constantly ached; we had covered the sixty-eight difficult miles of trail through the Smokies in only four days. Making matters worse, the cuff of my boot had irritated the Achilles tendon of my left leg, and, as I hobbled along, each step brought searing pain. I had been forced to walk in my running shoes, which provided little support, and I had tethered my boots—along with their five-pound heft—to my pack.

Then, there was the fatigue. Our systems seemed to be wearing down, and each day left us more tired than the previous day. In short, we were ready for a break. We had learned from a southbound hiker that Hot Springs was a five-star stop, and, in spite of our fatigue and my pestering leg pain, we pushed the last twenty-three miles into town in one day.

Once out of the woods, we arrived at the hiker hostel operated by the Jesuits, dumped our packs, and continued into town. The town of Hot Springs consists of a main street, an eighth-mile stretch of hardware shops, grocery stores, a laundromat, and a couple of cafes. Populated by farmers and mechanics in work clothes, it looks like any other small, southern, crossroads town. That is, until you spot the Inn.

As I neared the main intersection in town, I peered off to the right and through the trees spotted a magnificent two-story Victorian edifice painted white and appointed with a sharp-peaked roof, ornate columns, and a veranda that circled the entire second floor. The building—surrounded by gas stations, modest frame houses, and streets lined with rusting pickup trucks—would not have looked more out of place if it had been set on Fifth Avenue in New York City.

I stepped onto a covered porch, cluttered with bicycles and hanging plants, and opened the door into the kitchen. Inside, Elmer, clad in faded overalls and a flannel shirt and with a bushy salt-and-pepper beard, stood poised over an antique black cast-iron stove that spanned the wall opposite me. Randall stood by the sink, washing greens—onions, lettuce, and spinach—grown on his farm. Once in the room, I was enveloped in a cloud of savory aromas. Dill, curry, sage, and garlic wafted away from a quartet of pots simmering on the stove, mingling with the scent of bread baking in the oven. As I stood breathing the aroma, Elmer approached and welcomed me to the Inn. Then, Randall introduced himself.

After the greeting, Elmer invited me to explore the Inn, while the two returned to the task of preparing dinner for the twenty-plus hikers and other guests who would soon arrive for dinner.

I set out from the kitchen and made my way across a wood-paneled hallway and into a sitting room. The room had lost none of the Victorian charm it originally possessed when, near the turn of the century, the Inn catered to the wealthy clientele who journeyed to Hot Springs to bask in the town's natural mineral baths just two blocks away. A woven rug covered the hardwood floor, a wood-burning stove occupied the center of the room, and horse-hair couches and easy chairs nestled in corners next to antique tables and lamps. Original art from the 1920s hung between and above bookshelves that lined the walls. Many of the volumes were old leather-bound classics, and there were dozens of more modern coffee-table books of photography and art. But, most of the books were devoted to nature, religion, philosophy, travel, and adventure. As I scanned the shelves, the ethereal strains of one of Bach's Brandenburg concertos filled the room, reminding me of how much I had missed music while on the trail.

As I continued to explore, I found my way to the main dining room, outfitted with a half-dozen antique wooden tables and chairs. Two of the Inn's bedrooms opened off the main floor; the rest were upstairs. Most featured antique four-poster beds draped with patch-work quilts and doors leading out onto the veranda. At every turn, I encountered more books, and arrangements of fresh-cut spring flowers sat on tables in each room.

A room for the night cost eight dollars, and four dollars bought a four- or five-course vegetarian feast of gourmet soups, salads, breads, stews, and desserts—all made from scratch and served family-style. After our self-guided tour, Dan and I quickly retrieved our packs from the Jesuit hostel and took up lodging at the Inn.

Our first dinner there began, as all of them do, with a welcome from Elmer. After a brief prayer, he invited guests to introduce themselves to the group, and each hiker shared a bit of personal history and a general reaction to life on the trail. Then, the steam-ing platters of food arrived: spinach salad with vinaigrette dressing, black-bean soup, rice stew, whole-wheat bread, and fresh apple and berry pies, all hot from the oven. We washed it down with iced herbal tea.

After dinner, Elmer hosted a wine-tasting party, which drew a crowd of the artists and artisans—photographers, painters, poets, woodworkers—who had begun to settle in Hot Springs, turning it into a sort of backwoods Renaissance community with the Inn as its cultural epicenter. While Elmer entertained the more highbrow guests, Randall, whose cultural tastes were a shade folksier, hosted a collection of twelve hikers who lingered in the kitchen. The artists sipped wine and listened to classical music, while the rest of us pursued more down-home forms of amusement, sipping Tennessee whiskey and clogging to strains of mountain music from Randall's fiddle and the guitars of two of his friends. Soon, the cramped kitchen erupted into a regular hoedown, with hikers swinging arm in arm and stomping the floor with lug-soled boots.

Later that evening, when only Dan and I remained, Elmer suggested we take a drive; he wanted to show us something. We climbed into a rickety, decades-old Rambler and set off up the mountain. A few minutes later, we stopped at a pull-off on the quiet, two-lane highway and got out. Below us spread a scene of such stark beauty that I'll never forget it.

Several hundred yards below, miles away from the nearest incandescent light bulb, lay Randall's farm, its rolling fields shining silver in the moonlight. Above it rose the dark silhouettes of the mountains. In the center of the plot of cleared fields, a rustic two-room cabin sat on a hillside above a mountain brook. Moonbeams sliced through the skeleton of a rickety barn that stood beside it.

"We try to keep this place secret," said Elmer, "but it's so special that we like to share it with some of the people who come through town, who we think might appreciate it."

Randall went on to explain, in his thick Carolina drawl, that he had rented the farm several years earlier, and, since then, it had become his haven, his retreat, a place where he could pursue a simple, honest life of self-sufficiency that would keep him grounded in the Earth. The cabin had no electricity or running water, and he worked the farm without chemical pesticides or motorized tools, tilling the fields with a horse-drawn plow and spreading cow manure as organic fertilizer. Oil lamps provided evening light, and he warmed his dwelling and cooked over a wood-burning stove.

As we stood mesmerized by the scene, Elmer broke in. "We've really enjoyed the two of you, and we'd like for you to consider a proposition. If you need a few days' rest, we'd love to have you stay with us. You can help around the Inn or work on the farm for room and board, and you're welcome to stay as long as you like."

As far as I was concerned, there wasn't much deciding to be done. I needed rest, and the Inn and farm promised to expose me to a new way of life, one that my city upbringing had deprived me of. I voted to stay. Dan thought for a few seconds, then assented.

"This trail is about experiences," he said, "and I think there's a lot we could learn from this place."

So we took up residence in Hot Springs, like dozens of other hikers before and since who have wandered into town for a one-day stopover and wound up staying for days, weeks, or even years, living and learning from those two remarkable teachers.

And we did learn. For the next ten days, we shuttled between the Inn and the farm, working the fields through the morning and afternoon hours and in the evenings serving meals at the Inn. Each day brought new discoveries, new insights. For me, most of them occurred at Randall's farm, where I spent my nights, while Dan stayed at the Inn.

On the farm, mornings began at dawn with plates of hot beans and cornbread Randall had cooked on his stove. After breakfast, Dan and I, armed with hoes, acted as organic weed-killers, severing the necks of weeds that encroached on the tender, new sorghum sprigs. One day, as we hoed, Dan and I sang choruses of old African-American spirituals, the sun warming our shirtless backs. When the hoeing was done, we rode a horse-drawn cart, spreading manure along uncultivated fields that Randall would soon till behind Bill, his chestnut-brown workhorse.

Afternoons always ended with a hike up the mountainside to a spring-fed stream dammed into a series of cool, thigh-deep pools where, naked, we splashed the sweat and dirt from our bodies before walking to the Inn to serve the evening meal.

Mornings, I hovered close to Randall as he entered the barn and soothed his cow, Molly, pregnant and nearly ready to give birth. On Mother's Day morning, Randall summoned me to the barn, where Molly lay licking her limpid, gangly offspring, which Randall named Daisy. She had been born only minutes earlier, and, for the next several days, Molly's milk was rich yellow with colostrum, which tasted heavy and sweet.

Other days, I worked little, instead spending the day with a fishing pole, rock-hopping along the mountain brook spanned by the rickety, swinging bridge that separated Randall's spread from the quarter-mile dirt road that led to the highway.

Evenings were always special times. After we had finished our chores at the Inn, Elmer, Dan, and I walked or drove the three miles from the Inn to the rutted, quarter-mile dirt road that led back to the swinging bridge and Randall's farm. On one beautiful spring night, the four of us sat on the front porch of the cabin on a dilapidated car seat salvaged from an old Volkswagen. We filled metal cups with whiskey mixed with fresh mint leaves and cold spring water, dipped from an old barrel that sat on the side of the porch. A rubber hose led from a spring high up the mountain, down across a field and onto the porch, where it constantly infused the barrel with ice-cold water. The barrel, which was outfitted with a hinged door and a series of shelves, served as Randall's refrigerator. There he kept Molly's milk stored in a gallon glass jar.

That night at dusk, the sun burned like fire when it touched the ridge line, and it spread into a beautiful horizontal blaze of red, pink, and magenta. We had front-row seats for the pyrotechnics, and, after the sunlight began to fade, Randall took up his fiddle and, like a new-aged pied piper, led us out to the edge of the plowed field where he began scratching out the old Shaker hymn to encourage his crops to grow. Even today, when I hear the tune, I fondly recall my days in Hot Springs.

That night, after Elmer and Dan had returned to the Inn, Randall lit the stove to heat water for tea, and we sat down over the small kitchen table draped with an oilcloth. A single oil lamp illuminated the scarred, rough-hewn walls hung with mementos from Randall's life. There were Japanese watercolors from his travels to Asia to study Eastern religion during his years at Yale. There were photographs of his two sons, Randall, Jr., and Laird. There were mobiles crafted from bird bones or chips of quartz. There were shelves lined with hundreds of the knickknacks Randall had collected since moving to the farm: colorful stones, deer antlers, snakeskins, and turtle shells. They were, like the dwelling itself, beautifully austere, things most people would have swept aside to make room for more elegant furnishings. But, they were Randall's most prized possessions, and not one of them had cost him a cent.

We had grown very close over the previous few days, and I had begun to feel like a student in the presence of a wise teacher who instructed through precept and example without ever seeming to teach at all. Randall had a way of asking questions—thoughtful questions—that inspired introspection.

We had talked easily for a half-hour or so, sipping tea, when Randall staggered me with an ostensibly simple question that begged for a deeper response. "Will you share with me who you are?" I laughed, but I realized that it was a question I had been asking myself daily since I started the trail.

As I began to answer, I sensed that I was on the verge of a cathartic outpouring. For the next seven hours we talked, and it was the most honest, revealing, illuminating encounter I've ever had. I traced my history, not only exploring important events, but finding myself realizing for the first time the impact of those events, their meaning, how they had shaped me, led me in one direction or another, and how ultimately they had led me to the trail and here to Randall's farm.

As the night passed and Randall refilled our tea mugs, I shared things about myself that I had never broached before. I confessed. I voiced regrets. I expressed hopes. I talked about the kind of person I wanted to become: a person who loved and trusted more, a person who gave more, a person who fully appreciated life's simple blessings. As I spoke, I began to believe that such changes were possible.

I talked about the trail and how in three short weeks it had dazzled me and introduced me to a new world, one I had never imagined existed. A world full of goodness and beauty.

After I finished, I asked Randall the same question, and he shared his story with me. About the incompatible lifestyles that had divided him from his wife, she being drawn to the city, he to his primitive farm. About his sons, whom he loved desperately and saw too infrequently. He talked about his spiritual search that had led him to Yale and later to the Far East. About his entry into the ministry and the rejection that resulted when his New Age Christianity clashed with the fundamentalist values of his conservative neighbors. Finally, he talked about his decision to drop out, to abandon the mechanized world, and to sow his hopes for a better life here on the farm.

Near dawn, Randall rose from the table and put his arm around me, thanking me for the soul-deep dialogue we had shared. After bidding him goodnight and with an oil lamp in hand, I climbed the ladder to the open-air loft where I slept. Before settling to sleep, I extinguished the lamp and walked to the edge of the loft, which looked out over the silent fields and shadowed mountains. The evening chill felt clean and good against my face, and I watched the steam of my breath billow and fade. Beyond, I could see the dew twinkling in the moonlight, and I detected the faint smell of manure, the sweet bite of hay, the perfume of clover. The rich tang of wood smoke hung in the air, and I heard Molly and her new calf lowing softly in the barn. I heard the water lapping over the stones in the stream. Suddenly, the boundaries separating me from the tranquil night world disappeared. The mountains engulfed me, and I began to feel as if I had just been born into a world filled with peace.

I experienced such an intense swell of emotion that I could hardly contain it, and, for the first time in my life, I knew that God and all His goodness dwelt in every rock, in every tree, in every blade of grass, and in me. I walked to the mattress, climbed under the quilt, and lay—awake—until dawn, fearful that, if I slept, I would awaken to find the feelings gone.

But, several days later, when Dan and I said good-bye to Elmer and Randall and departed Hot Springs on May 19, those feelings were still as surely connected to me as my pack and walking stick. From then on, the trail seemed different—more inviting, more filled with wonder, more charged with excitement. And, as we picked up the white blazes, heading north, I realized that what I had discovered in Hot Springs was just the beginning. Hundreds of miles lay ahead, miles full of promise.

CHAPTER ELEVEN

Critters

I'm learning that nature can he as harsh as it is beautiful. I watched tonight as Randall's cat crept up into the open loft of the cabin, crouched, and uncoiled, seizing a bat that had been fluttering around the rafters in the lantern light. The cat then walked past me down the ladder with the bat still wriggling in her jaws. The act was so quick, so efficient, and yet so horrifying to me, perhaps because I haven't watched many living things die. Afterward, it occurred to me that predators like the cat are playing out their roles in this theater without malice or spite or cruelty, which we humans tend to ascribe to them and their killing acts.

MAY 16, 1979
RANDALL'S FARM
HOT SPRINGS, NORTH CAROLINA

N MANY WAYS, THE APPALACHIAN TRAIL WAS A THRIV-ing biology lab or, more precisely, a biology theater where myriad critters—many I had no idea existed—bustled, stirred, buzzed, tittered, slithered, and scrambled about, entertaining and educating us with their antics. Through them, we received a first-hand survival lesson.

But, the animals offered us more than that. Over time, they became our colleagues, appealing to our sense of sight or sound through all of our days and nights on the trail and reminding us always that man, the animal, is never alone, never wanting for companions. There was the screech of the pileated woodpecker winging unseen through densely foliated tree tops. Graceful hawks and buzzards spiraled effortlessly on thermals. Barred owls or wild turkeys glided agilely on four-foot wings through dense hardwood forests. Woodchucks, chipmunks, and squirrels rummaged through the underbrush for seeds or insect larvae. Skunks sauntered slowly across the trail with their young in tow.

There was the collective drone of millions of insects—the rhythmic tweep of crickets, the rasp of cicadas, the oscillating buzz of bumblebees weaving through the underbrush. The flutelike trill of the brown thrush and the incessant banter of the whip-poor-will violated the sanctity of night, and we could hear the tapping and pawing of white-tailed deer as they foraged through open meadows after dark.

In our daily and nightly encounters with the animals, it became difficult not to view them as paradigms, as living symbols of simplicity, contentment, and clarity of purpose in the often charitable, sometimes hostile, world of the wilderness. For the animals, to live was enough. Whitman captured that sentiment so well in *Leaves of Grass*:

> I think I could turn and live with animals,
> they are so placid and self-contained,
> I stand and look at them long and long.
> They do not sweat and whine about their condition,

They do not lie awake in the dark and weep
    for their sins,
They do not make me sick discussing their duty to
    God.
Not one is dissatisfied, not one is demented with the
    mania of owning things,
Not one kneels to another nor to his kind that lived
    thousands of years ago,
Not one is respectable or unhappy over the whole
    Earth.

I saw my first black bear in the Smokies, as I hiked alone from Ice Water Springs to Cosby Knob in the northern section of the national park. He was a great three-year-old male, and he sat in the middle of the trail with his feet splayed outward, back erect, like a Buddha in brown fur. Placid and self-contained, he seemed to embody the spirit of Whitman's tribute.

When I first spotted him, I wanted to shout, to share my excitement with my companions behind me on the trail, but I realized that to do so would have sent the animal fleeing through the trees. Instead, I stood trembling, like an adolescent who has just discovered sex, studying the bear as he swept the branches of a small bush into his gaping mouth.

The bear wasn't beautiful, and he wasn't majestic. In fact, he was somewhat waggish, with his abundant fat and baggy skin draped around him like an outsized black overcoat and with a vacant, blissful expression spread across his face. But, he was also astonishing, because he was there at all: a massive wild beast pursuing his simple livelihood not forty yards in front of me.

After two minutes, I ventured closer and snapped his photograph. Because I was positioned downwind, his powerful sense of smell—many times more acute than my own—didn't register my scent, and he was left to evaluate me through his rather feeble eyesight. After scrutinizing me for several seconds, he showed no alarm and remained where he sat until he had eaten his fill and decided to move on. I followed his clamorous passage down the mountain by tracing the heavy thud of his footfalls and the rustle of snapping branches.

When he was gone, I felt blessed to have been permitted such an intimate glimpse of one of North America's largest creatures, and I realized that our encounter was vastly more honest, more revealing, than ever might have occurred in a zoo. He and I had met on equal terms. No fences separated us; no man-made walls sealed him in or kept him out. He was free to roam as he pleased, freer in many ways than I, who adhered to established trails while he, guided by whim or instinct, created his own.

Taken alone, the encounter with the bear was enough to thrill me for weeks, but it was only one of three major wildlife sightings I had logged over the previous few days.

Two days earlier, I had stood within ten yards of a six-point buck. I had left my backpack on the ridge at Spence Field, at five thousand feet, and had wandered down a sunlit trail to fill my water bottle at a spring. As the chilly water tumbled over my hands, I heard a twig snap and looked up to see him peering at me.

My heart pounded as I watched him, certain that at any moment he would spook and vanish through the trees. But, he never did. After several minutes, he strayed away at an easy pace, rooting for acorns as he went.

Then, there were the wild boars. As I ascended from Spence Field toward the summit of Thunderhead late in the afternoon, I peered ahead to see an ample brown rump disappear into the brush. An eighth of a mile farther up the trail, I glanced thirty yards below me and saw an entire herd of twelve to fourteen wild boars—from three-hundred-pound sows to cat-sized piglets—scampering through a thicket. I later learned that the boars were descendants of the Russian wild boars introduced to the area in 1910 by a lodge keeper who had imported them to serve as game for his clientele. The boars proved an elusive quarry, and the hunting lodge soon closed its doors, but the animals went on to thrive in the park.

Later that evening, when I reached Derrick Knob Shelter— six miles north—I met a ranger on horseback. Slung over his shoulder was a shotgun mounted with a spotlight. He was boar hunting, part of a park-wide effort to eradicate the animals, which already had destroyed acres of foliage by rooting for acorns with their tusks. Above three thousand feet, the ranger would drag his kill off the trail and leave it as food for the carrion-eaters.

HROUGH THE SPRING AND SUMMER, THE RUFFED grouse also became an important woodland symbol and a perfect emblem of the passing of the seasons. The game birds were always willing to share the secrets of their life cycle and their tactics of self-preservation with any passerby willing to look and listen.

I heard the birds long before I first glimpsed them. On our second night on the trail, for instance, I heard an eerie drumming sound that resembled the noise of a basketball being dribbled with increasing tempo on a carpeted floor. I heard that sound again and again over the next few days, yet neither Dan nor I had the slightest notion of what it was. We learned later that the dribbling sound arose from a male ruffed grouse, beating the air with its wings to attract a mate.

Several days later, as I ambled along a tranquil stretch of trail lost in thought, a sudden explosion of thundering wings jarred me to attention. Out of the corner of my eye, I spotted two birds the size of large game hens beating their wings and flying erratically through the trees. Their black, brown, and tan feathers provided perfect camouflage, and, when they lit in trees several hundred feet away, they virtually disappeared into the background colors of the wilderness.

As the weeks passed, I found myself repeatedly startled by the grouse. Even though I encountered them every few days, I never learned to anticipate their frenetic, graceless retreat. Yet, with each encounter, I learned more about them. I soon learned, for instance, that, when spooked, the male fled to a faraway tree, while the hen stayed near the nest. Though separated by some distance, the two birds maintained a constant communication of staccato squawks, perhaps a verbal assessment of their two-legged intruder. I also found that, if I ignored their decoy and instead located the now-abandoned nest, I could glimpse tiny, perfectly camouflaged chicks darting for cover in the underbrush.

One day as I walked along the trail through the Blue Ridge of Virginia, I encountered a nest and, as usual, the male grouse scattered while the female clung to the ground. When she noticed that I had spied the nest, she employed her first diversionary tactic, which no doubt was intended to decoy predators. She hopped onto the trail in front of me, staggering drunkenly and feigning a broken wing. When she looked back and realized that I had called her bluff, she shifted to her second tactic, one that I still regard as the most perfect act of selfless devotion I've ever seen. Now twenty feet ahead on the trail, she turned to face me and billowed out her feathers until she had doubled in size. Squawking maniacally, she charged.

I held my position as the protective mother approached, but, when she began nipping at my legs with her beak and thrashing me with her wings, I suddenly found myself fleeing down the trail—more amazed than afraid—with the enraged hen in hot pursuit.

As the spring yielded to summer, the chicks continued to grow with each sighting. By summer's end, the chaos of dozens of thrashing wings greeted me whenever I encountered a nest, with father, mother, and offspring together taking wing in retreat.

THER BIRDS HAD ADAPTED MORE GRACIOUSLY TO our presence and approached rather than withdrew from us. While I hiked through the Green Mountains of Vermont, for instance, one day I stopped in a spruce grove to have a snack. Pulling a granola bar from my pack, I sat on a rock, but no sooner had I peeled off the wrapper than a gray Canada jay landed squarely on my shoulder. At first, I suspected that I had been visited by a winged demon, but soon the jay roosted on my finger and nibbled from my hand.

Through the North Woods, the plump, round-headed birds, also known as scavenger jays or camp jays, became invited dinner guests and even entertainers. On the last night of our hike, in the twin shelters at Katahdin Stream Campground, one hiker in our group plugged both of his nostrils with bread, lay on his back, and soon catered a buffet for two jays. While the birds roosted on his chin and picked the bread from his nose, the rest of us howled, more shocked by the behavior of our own species than by that of the animals.

The jays were perhaps the most loveable among the camp raiders that abounded on the trail. The others engaged us in a never-ending battle of wits, but, while we often disdained their efforts to pillage our supplies, we also marveled at their pluck and adaptability. They had learned to regard humans as hosts, not intruders.

Mice. When Dante described the inferno, rife with fire and darkness, he omitted one detail: mice. Millions of them, with rasping teeth and clattering claws.

I had my first encounter with mice on my third night on the trail. I had slept beside my foodbag in the shelter, certain that no creature would venture close to a sleeping human. I awoke to find a quarter-sized hole leading through the green nylon and into each of the half-dozen plastic bags inside. As it turned out, the stealthy mice had sampled from the bags, mingling their tiny brown droppings with the contents of each. The next night, I hung my foodbag from a nail driven into a shelter eave, thinking I had surely outsmarted them. I awoke the next morning to discover new ports of entry and freshly laid turds.

Determined to observe the rapscallions at work, the next night I lay in my bag, gripping my flashlight. As soon as I blew out the candle, the frantic chorus of scraping and gnawing began. The more brazen shelter denizens crisscrossed the shelter eaves, and, when I clicked on my flashlight, their tiny eyes glowed red in the beam. Finally, one reached the nail that supported my foodbag and scampered down the line. Now in the spotlight, he gnawed insouciantly at the nylon until I drove him away with a well-aimed stone.

I was baffled and prepared to offer nightly sacrifices—small heaps of food—in hopes that the mice would leave the larger portion alone. The next day, a more experienced hiker taught me how to pierce a tuna can in the center, invert it, and suspend it midway along the line to discourage even the most enterprising rodents.

The barrier prevented them from reaching my food, but I soon discovered that the mice did more than assail food-bags. Once they realized our edible supplies were beyond their reach, they turned their sights on our wool socks and shirts and even raided our rolls of toilet tissue. The shredded tissue and frayed wool provided soft, warm batting for their dens, and close inspection between the shelter logs almost always revealed cushy nests heaped in colored wool and white tissue.

We soon learned to leave the pockets of our packs unzipped, to allow the critters free access. Otherwise, their teeth would have made quick work of the pack cloth if a pocket contained so much as a crumb of bread or a single rolled-oat flake. I awoke one morning in a shelter to find a trio of rigid mouse tails projecting from flaps and pocket openings, and when I picked up my pack no fewer than a dozen mice leaped for safety Thankfully, because I had left the pockets open, they had left my pack intact, though liberally sprinkled with feces.

Though personal assaults were rare, they were not unheard of. The night we slept at Sassafrass Gap Shelter, seven miles north of Wesser, North Carolina, one of the other shelter occupants woke us all with a shout in the wee hours of the morning. A mouse had blazed a path across his forehead, stopped near his nose, and emptied its tiny bladder into his eye. And, it wasn't unusual for an errant mouse to take a wrong turn and wind up inside a bag occupied by a slumbering hiker, an accident that usually resulted in a chorus of squeaks and shrieks as man and beast scrambled to escape their odd bedfellow.

While most of us faced the mouse menace with resignation and even good-natured fascination, others devised grim methods for reprisal. One hiker, for instance, carried a supply of traps that he rigged each night before he turned in. Within minutes of lights out, we would hear the clatter of spring-loaded jaws; the hiker then slipped from his bag, tossed the casualties out into the brush, and started the process over again.

Everyone soon began to consider his pesticidal mission an exercise in futility. The mice were so populous that, while a few strayed into the traps, dozens of others pillaged the shelter with impunity. Before abandoning his calling altogether, however, the hiker resorted to more drastic measures. He rigged a tiny hangman's noose and suspended a dead mouse from the rafters in a Virginia shelter, a warning to others that they might suffer the same fate. His mouse lynching, like his efforts with the traps, backfired, and he soon found himself besieged not only by mice but also by fellow hikers who considered his tactics cruel and inhumane.

In the war against the mice, it seems the best we could hope for was a truce: If we stashed our socks and shirts and hung our foodbags properly, the mice contented themselves with the scraps spilled from our dinner pots.

Some shelters harbored larger, more daunting scavengers. Ice Water Springs Shelter in the Smokies, for instance, served as home to a resident skunk. While I slept in the shelter on the bottom tier of wire-mesh bunks two feet above the ground, I awoke at 3:00 a.m. to see the skunk's tail passing inches from my nose as he scoured the floor for food.

One evening in the Shenandoah National Park, Dan and I camped in an open field, and, shortly after dark, we heard a frantic rustling at the base of the tree that bore our food-bags. We soon trained our flashlights on an enterprising raccoon who spent the better part of the night devising tactics to reach our food, which dangled from a stout bough fifteen feet above the ground. First, the animal tried to untie the knot that secured the cord to the tree trunk. When that failed, he scampered up the tree and worked at the line where it draped over the branch. Finally, he suspended himself from the limb, grabbed at the line, and set the bags swinging back and forth. Though the animal never reached the foodbags, I had to resist a temptation to reward him for his perseverance and cunning.

Raccoons weren't the only animals that employed ingenious techniques. In the Smokies, a park ranger related a story about a notorious camp-raider known as the Suicide Bear. The bear was known for hoisting himself into trees and, like a portly trapeze artist, flinging himself in the direction of the dangling foodbags. More often than not, the ranger explained, the bear would crash to the ground empty-handed. Undaunted, he would scale the tree and leap again and again until finally, bruised and battered, he limped off into the woods.

Occasionally, his plan worked. He would leap, snatch the food bag in his paws, cling to it until the line snapped, and then scamper off into the brush with his pilfered dinner. According to the ranger, the bear's fur was a mass of scabs and bald patches, but he also sported an ample layer of fat, proof that his leaps into the void were sometimes productive.

Vermont was porcupine country, and the scavengers' teethmarks scarred everything that bore a trace of salt from hikers' sweat. The sharp edges of shelter planking, forest service signs, and even outhouse seats had been gnawed smooth. Pack straps, boots, and walking sticks posed equally tempting morsels, and we hung them along with our foodbags. Though I never saw a porcupine, the gnarled wood and piles of stones—antiporcupine artillery—left in shelters attested to bitter night battles between hikers and the bristling marauders.

HE ANIMALS' BEHAVIOR PATTERNS WEREN'T ALWAYS as endearing as those of the grouse or as comical as those of the camp raiders, particularly when they embraced the harsh and sometimes gruesome world of predators and prey.

Near the streambed of Sages Ravine in Connecticut, for in-

AS FAR AS THE EYE CAN SEE

stance, I watched, horrified, as yellow jackets descended on a butterfly in such numbers that they completely obscured the body, covered the wings, and swarmed over the ground in a wriggling mass two feet in diameter. Initially, the butterfly struggled, but, within seconds, the battle was over. As the predators continued to work, the dead insect's wings waved pathetically as the wasps' mandibles gnawed through the tissue that attached the wings to the body. Perhaps the butterfly had strayed too close to the nest, or maybe the yellow jackets had sought him as food to be chewed to pulp and fed to their larvae.

In Virginia, I watched a giant cicada killer, a two-inch-long wasp with a bulbous, gold-spotted abdomen, swoop onto a cicada that clung to a tree trunk. The wasp arched its abdomen and drove in its stinger. When the cicada had stopped twitching, the insect dropped with its prey to the ground. It then lumbered into the air, still clutching its victim and flying like an overloaded transport plane to its den, where, I learned, it would lay its eggs on the body of the paralyzed host. When the eggs hatched, the larve would enter the body of the cicada and eat the insect alive from the inside.

During my stay at Randall's farm in Hot Springs, North Carolina, I witnessed another staggering display of predatory skill. Nights at the cabin, I slept in an open-air loft with no walls separating me from the night air. One evening, as I poked my head through the trap door leading to the loft, I spotted a bat swooping through the open space under the eaves. An oil lamp dangled from my hand, and, from its position below the trap door, it infused the loft with a faint, eerie glow.

As I watched the bat zig and zag along the rafters of the open room, Randall's tailless cat, Ichtar, slipped up the ladder, brushed past my chest, and crept onto the floor beside my head. Her body remained still while her head swiveled, tracking the bat's erratic course.

Though I had no idea what was about to happen, I was transfixed by the scene: a domesticated cat, but a predator, crouching, silhouetted against the dark walls of the loft, while the bat, seemingly drawn to the new life presence in the room, swooped closer with each pass. Finally, the bat flew within striking distance, and Ichtar's body uncoiled with such force and quickness that I missed the motion completely.

Still perched on the ladder, I lifted the lamp onto the loft floor and saw that the cat held the wriggling bat in her jaws. She moved back down the ladder, brushing past my chest, as serenely and purposefully as when she had arrived, while I, with racing heart and trembling hands, felt unnerved, as if I had just witnessed a murder.

Miles farther south, in Georgia, I had experienced a similar pang of disgust and frustration after I witnessed a suicide. Four of us sat by a fire and noticed a pale green luna moth—as large as a small bird—swooping close to the flames. Having watched count-less insects scorch themselves in our candle flames, we knew what was likely to follow. While we had had little concern for the self-destructive bent of smaller, less spectacular insects, the imminent self-immolation of the luna provoked a response in all of us. We rose, flailing our arms attempting to block the insect's path back to the fire. But, our protective efforts posed little deterrent for the moth, and it easily maneuvered past us.

Inexorably programmed on its suicidal mission, the insect sput-tered through the flames and careened to the ground on the far side of the fire. Mortally wounded, it lay on its back, wriggling its seared legs and fluttering its singed wings until it had righted itself. No longer able to fly, it limped along the ground, scaled one of the rocks ringing the fire, and heaved itself into the pyre. There, without apparent fear or despair, it vanished in a brilliant flash of green flame.

CHAPTER TWELVE

Where I Live

I believe I have finally found my niche, and it's here in the woods. I thrive here. I relax here. I feel so right here. And, I've begun to realize that I have become a resident of the wilderness: I no longer leave society to visit the woods. Rather, I leave the woods to visit society. When I'm in town, I feel uprooted and often suffer pangs of separation. When I'm in town, I constantly wonder what natural displays I'm missing, and it's also sometimes difficult to sleep, because the air seems stale and all the familiar night sounds are muted by walls and windows.

AUGUST 77, 1979
LITTLE ROCK POND LEAN-TO, VERMONT

 **ONE OF US WHO VENTURED OUT ON THE APPALACHIAN** Trail for weeks at a time could resist being transformed by the experience.

Some of the changes were obvious. "There's something different about thru-hikers," Richard Bramley, the owner of a package store on the trail in Cornwall

Bridge, Connecticut, once told me. Bramley, who offers free drinks to thru-hikers, has spent hours on his front porch listening to the stories of end-to-enders. "Once you've spent over two or three weeks on the trail, you're into a different head. You've begun to change. You've left the rest of the world behind, and it shows." People like Bramley who frequently encounter thru-hikers claim there is an unmistakable aura about them, a lean, hard look and a beatific demeanor.

Our clothes were perpetually soiled and often tattered, and the backs of our T-shirts bore permanent gray streaks where the aluminum crossbars of our packs had oxidized. Our boots were scuffed and scarred by rocks and roots, and our hair and beards grew unencumbered. By the time I reached Maine, for instance, I could no longer negotiate a comb through the tangle that billowed from my face.

Our leg muscles became sharply defined, and whatever fat we had carried along the early miles through the South soon disappeared. We covered miles—whether climbing or descending—at the same brisk, three-mile-per-hour pace. On long ascents, we frequently blazed by weekend hikers who swore and grunted their way to the top. Our packs truly looked like mobile homes, with socks, bandannas, and surplus shorts and T-shirts tethered to the outside to dry in the sun.

Other changes were more subtle. After weeks on the trail, primitive instincts began to awaken. Away from the bombardment of loud music and the din of rush-hour traffic, our hearing became sensitized to the gentle cues of the wilderness. Never silent, the woods were constantly astir with the titter of birds, the rustle of wind through the leaves, the scurry of chipmunks scattering through the underbrush, the drone of buzzing insects, the rumble of distant thunder clouds, the crackling of approaching footsteps.

We developed a knack for predicting changes in the weather. By reading shifting winds, cloud formations, subtle changes in pressure, or the smell of dampness in the air, we could often forecast impending storms hours before they struck.

At the same time, the sounds, smells, and sensations of civilization became foreign and at times even threatening to us. The clamor of trucks and cars streaking along highways contrasted so starkly to the sounds of the woods, for instance, that I became edgy whenever the trail crossed a main road.

Other sounds pitched me into panic. I recall the night we camped beside Pierce Pond in the wilderness of central Maine, miles from the nearest road. I had finished my dinner and had climbed out onto a large rock that jutted into the water. As I lay on my back, gazing contentedly at the night sky, I dozed into a tranquil sleep, only to be jarred awake as a fighter jet from Pease Air Force Base a few hundred miles away roared across the lake at treetop level, shooting flames from its afterburners. The incident left me shaken and disoriented, unable to sleep.

Other, less invasive, aspects of civilization disturbed us, too. The stench of car exhaust burned our nostrils as we descended into towns from the fresh, clean air of the mountains, and the odors of perfume, deodorant, and soap on the well-scrubbed people we encountered in towns almost sickened us at times. In one instance, I was positioned in a line of a dozen tourists in a grocery check-out aisle in Rangeley, Maine, when the collective assault of a dozen bottled fragrances left me wondering if I could clear the register and exit with my supplies before I gagged. I suspect that my own rank aroma left my fellow shoppers wondering the same thing.

We could smell the acrid odor of tobacco smoke ahead of us on the trail from as far as a quarter-mile away. We also began to notice that day-hikers carried on their clothes the distinct odor of their houses and the foods they had cooked for dinner. Often, as they passed me on the trail, I instinctively raised my nose to the air, reading their scents on the wind.

There were other changes, too. Over my five months on the trail, the very rhythm of my life settled down. I had no deadlines, no commitments, no job awaiting my return, no schedule to keep beyond reaching Maine before my cash reserves ran dry. I ate when I was hungry, slept when I was tired, hiked alone when I felt crowded or with friends when I felt lonely. I rose at dawn and covered my daily mileage with ample time to tarry at mountaintop vistas or soak my feet in streams and still make camp with enough daylight to roll out my bag, boil my noodles, write in my journal, and brew my evening cup of tea before sunset. My wristwatch became just another trinket to weigh me down and clutter my life, and I sent it home. Today, if I could revive any element of the trail experience, it would be that wonderful feeling of escape from mechanized timekeeping and the sense that the daylight hours provided more than ample time for fulfilling my obligations.

But, the most notable change in me was the evolution from visitor to resident of the wilderness. It was such a gradual change that I can't say exactly when or where it happened, and I tried to explain it to Victor, the Massachusetts hiker who had departed the trail in North Carolina and joined us for weekends as we passed through New England. On an afternoon hike through the Green Mountains of Vermont, he asked me what it was like to spend so many days away from civilization. As we walked through a fir grove, across exposed rock outcroppings, up boulder-strewn climbs, and finally to camp beside a tumbling brook, I explained that I felt as if I were ushering him through my home the way someone might walk a visitor through his house, pointing to the kitchen where he ate his meals, to the den where he sat with his evening tea, to the bedroom where he slept.

I explained to him that my layovers in town had become progressively shorter, and that I quickly became "homesick" for the woods. I told him that, for every minute I dallied in town, I realized that I chanced missing the natural wonders occurring in the mountains: hawks circling on thermals, bears lumbering away in retreat, scavenger Canada jays eating from my hand, deer pawing through camp at dusk, stellar sunsets rippling the horizon in waves of purple, red, and blue, and golden meteors blazing across black night skies that always left me with goose bumps no matter how many times I had seen them.

I explained to him that many of the trappings of my life in the city—electric can openers, microwave ovens, television sets, blow-driers, daily hot showers—seemed excessive, wasteful. I explained that I had lost my lust for material things and could not think of anything I really wanted that wasn't already in my pack.

If the wilderness was my home, then many of the trail's 230 shelters served as my domiciles, linking passage through fourteen states and the 160 days of my trek. I could never resist the thrill of counting down the day's last mile, of feeling my pace quicken in anticipation, and finally glancing ahead and spotting the blue-blazed side trail or the shelter roof through the trees and knowing that the day's labor was complete, that it was time to rest.

The shelters were spartan, fifteen-by-ten-foot open-faced lean-tos with sloping roofs and fieldstone walls or walls hewn from native timbers. Some of the shelters were spectacular relics of the 1930s, of the trail's earliest days and of the craftsmanship of the Civilian Conservation Corps. Some, like the squat Cable Gap Shelter seven miles south of the entrance to the Great Smoky Mountains National Park, were constructed of stout, two-foot-broad logs. A few of the shelters boasted four, not three, walls and included doorways, lofts, and shuttered windows. The Roan High Knob Shelter on the shoulder of Roan Mountain and the Blood Mountain Shelter, thirty miles north of Springer, were two such places.

Many shelters perched on the ridgeline and afforded spectacular views of the surrounding mountains. Vandeventer Shelter, for instance, rests on a rocky ridge some one thousand feet above Watauga Dam, thirty-three miles south of the Virginia border. During our night on the ridge, we watched as the daylight waned and tiny lights shimmered like earth-bound stars, each marking a house or a barn or a church. The next morning, we awoke to find the lake and her civilization gone. Instead, we saw a stratus of dense silver clouds probed by the round green knobs of surrounding mountains.

Other shelters—Ice Water Springs, Russell Field, Spence Field, Derrick Knob, all in the Smokies—were crafted of fieldstone and equipped with indoor hearths and fireplaces.

Some, particularly those through the Lake Country of central

Maine, nestled alongside pristine ponds whose treelined shores were scattered with rocks and driftwood bleached white in the sun. There, the wild, maniacal laughter of loons echoed across the still water after dark.

Though simple, those accommodations afforded us more pleasure than a welter of more extravagant, more civilized offerings ever could. A roof to keep off the rain. Three walls to block the wind. A timber platform on which to sleep or sit and watch the gradual arrival of nightfall. A sixteen-penny nail driven into the shelter eaves, a place to hang damp shorts, a waterbag, or a parcel of food. A spiral-bound register filled with pages and pages of hikers' tales, experiences, reflections, insights. A nearby spring spouting delicious, fifty-degree water. A stout tree to cradle one's back.

Once at the shelter, I would slip from my sweat-soaked clothes and wander to the spring to fill my waterbag and splash the day's grime from my skin. Then, I would pull on a pair of dry socks, a clean cotton T-shirt and wool shirt, a pair of long trousers, and a pair of ragged sneakers that seemed to weigh nothing at all after a day in hiking boots. If it was early in the evening, I might have four or five hours of daylight to do exactly as I pleased: to write, to read, to feed the fire, to talk with friends, to explore the environs of my temporary home. Or, to do nothing at all and feel that the time was just as well spent.

CHAPTER THIRTEEN

Special Attractions

Talk of mysteries! Think of our life in nature—daily to be shown matter, to come in contact with it—rocks, trees, wind on our cheeks! The solid Earth!

HENRY DAVID THOREAU
THE MAINE WOODS

EFORE ASSAULTING SPRINGER MOUNTAIN, I HAD heard or read accounts of the trail's "special attractions," those sections that possessed the grandest vistas, posed the most grueling ascents or descents, harbored the largest and most varied populations of wildlife, boasted the most exhilarating traverses, or offered other qualities that made them especially memorable to hikers.

For the northbounder, the trail seems to arrange those sections in perfect sequence. As hikers move north and develop physical and mental stamina, they encounter progressively more demanding terrain and more challenging experiences.

It begins with Springer Mountain, an unremarkable peak, really, at just over three thousand feet and shrouded in hardwood trees. For thru-hikers, the mountain ranks as a major milestone, marking either the outset or completion of their months-long trek.

Some 165 miles farther north, hikers enter the Great Smoky Mountains National Park, which teems with wildlife—bears, boars, skunks, deer. As the most frequently visited national park in the country, it teemed with human life, too. Through the park, we ascended through rhododendron groves, along cascading brooks tangled in dense, rich underbrush, and across bald-topped mountains, and we scaled the tallest peak on the entire trail, Clingmans Dome, at 6,643 feet.

The 106 miles through Virginia's Shenandoah National Park led us through open meadows and over rocky promontories. In other places through Virginia, we traced the trail over centuries-old carriage ruts past abandoned homesteads and settlements where flower gardens still blossom and cherry and apple trees still yield fruit.

Much farther north, six and one-half miles beyond the Maine–New Hampshire border, the Mahoosuc Notch offers a mile-long scramble under, around, and between bus-sized boulders. The Notch is regarded as the trail's toughest mile, but I regarded it as a gray, lichen-covered amusement park where we followed a series of white arrows that marked the only route through the jumble of granite blocks. The tight passages through the rocks frequently required us to shed our packs, tie them with parachute cord, and trail them behind us as we wedged through the cracks and fissures. Midway through the notch, we stopped to rest and dipped our drinking cups into a spring that courses under the rocks. As I withdrew my cup, the sides immediately fogged with condensation, even though the air temperature hovered in the fifties, and, when I touched the cup to my mouth, the water was so frigid that it stung my lips.

Those were all special places, yet the trail offered three sections that, for me, represented emotional or aesthetic highlights of my trek: the White Mountains of New Hampshire, with their barren, windswept ridges that reach above timberline with the stark grandeur of the Swiss Alps; the Kennebec River, in southwestern Maine, an optional ford across 150 feet of roiling, waist-deep rapids; and Mount Katahdin, the lone granite sentry that rises out of the Lake Country of central Maine and which I regard as the trail's most perfect mountain.

The White Mountains

We have been blessed with beautiful weather for our passage along the Franconia and Presidential ridges, where the trail reaches above treeline. Having heard descriptions of the rawer aspects of the weather in these mountains—and of the deaths that have resulted—we're both relieved and grateful. Crossing the Whites in fog, sleet, summer snows, dangerous winds, or any combination of those things would have made for tough going, but the worst part would have been exploring these mountains without being able to see them. We had heard that the terrain is challenging here, and I suppose that it has been, but I've been too absorbed in the grandeur and beauty that greets us at every turn even to notice.

AUGUST 30, 1979
LAKES OF THE CLOUDS HUT
WHITE MOUNTAINS, NEW HAMPSHIRE

On April 12, 1934, the weather station on the barren summit of Mount Washington clocked winds in excess of 230 miles per hour, the stiffest winds ever recorded at a manned weather station. To put that figure into perspective, hurricane-force winds begin at seventy-five miles per hour. As the story goes, after the incredulous meteorologist confirmed the reading, the gauge broke, and winds continued to gain in intensity.

The winds and harsh winter weather have sculpted the ancient granite of the Whites into vast bowls, cirques, and windswept ridges stripped bare of all plant life but scrub vegetation, alpine flowers, and tundra grass. Along Franconia Ridge and through the Presidential Range, the trail lopes above timberline and often stays there for miles, crossing the summits of Mount Lincoln (5,089 feet), Mount Lafayette (5,249), Mount Jackson (4,052), Mount Pierce (4,310), Mount Eisenhower (4,761), Mount Franklin (5,004), Mount Washington (6,288), and Mount Madison (5,363).

For most of us who had passed the previous 1,700 miles cloaked in hardwood forests and shrouded in lush vegetation, our first forays above timberline seemed accompanied by magic. For every wonderful vista we had enjoyed through the twelve states leading from Georgia to Vermont, we had scrambled over hundreds of less spectacular peaks that, day after day, offered no vistas, no break from the often monotonous routine of ascents and descents. The Whites were different—in fact, majestic, a term I would be reluctant to apply to any of the other ranges we passed through *en route*. They were majestic because their stately summits towered as many as three thousand feet above treeline and provided unbroken, panoramic vistas in every direction.

The terrain above timberline boasts exaggerated proportions, where mountains swell like barren, well-muscled biceps; where clouds don't float, but shoot across the sky like ice splinters; and where the wind assaults you in sudden gusts that tug at your watch cap, billow your parka and pants, and leave you tottering and lurching for balance. Above timberline, the absence of trees scrambles your sense of distance and size. Open vistas make a dozen miles appear like a few hundred yards until you spot another hiker, a tiny black form advancing along a gargantuan crest, and your perspective returns and you begin to feel as small as the distant hiker appears.

Above timberline, the trails themselves meld into the Hobbit-like landscape. You can glimpse ahead a mile, five miles, ten miles, and follow the serpentine cut of the trail as it meanders across ridges, slumps into saddles, skirts around peaks, disappears, then emerges again as it strays back into your line of sight. The trails snake to the horizon, becoming ever more faint, narrowing with the distance, and you walk them with your eyes before you explore them with your feet. Ahead, you can see where you will stand in one hour, two hours, a day.

At the same time, the scale turns the landscape into a living relief map, and hiking becomes a lesson in living geography. You begin to understand how one peak links to the next, how streams follow the folds in the ridges and converge into rivers.

Our days along Franconia Ridge and through the Presidential Range to the summit of Mount Washington were marked by blue skies and moderate temperatures. We visited several of the high-elevation huts operated by the Appalachian Mountain Club (AMC), which provide lodging and gourmet meals for short-term hikers who may spend several days to a week in the Whites, but none of us had the cash to pay the twenty dollars per night. Often we arrived at the huts just after breakfast and gobbled up left-over whole-wheat pancakes and muffins at five cents apiece.

On August 30, we reached Lakes of the Clouds Hut, a rustic T-shaped lodge sided with weathered cedar shakes. This, the largest of the AMC's eight huts, accommodates as many as ninety guests. Though we couldn't afford to pay for dinner and a bunk, the hut crew members allowed us to sleep on table tops in the dining room for two dollars. The next morning, the sun glinted through the windows, and we knew we were in for a beautiful summit day. Along the 1.4 miles to the top, we battled forty-mile-per-hour winds, which formed horizontal spikes of rime ice on the windward sides of trail signs and rocks, but the day remained clear. As we soon discovered, not everyone who explored the mountain had been so fortunate.

The same features that render the alpine ridges of the Whites majestic also make them deadly. Days earlier, as we neared the top of the three-thousand-foot ascent leading from Franconia Notch to the ridge, we confronted the first of several yellow warning signs posted at timberline. They read: "Attention: Try this trail only if you are in top physical condition, well clothed, and carrying extra clothing and food. Many have died above timberline from exposure. Turn back at the first sign of bad weather." The conditions are particularly harsh on Mount Washington. Later, I would learn that the average June temperature on the mountain is forty-five degrees; in July, it's forty-nine; and in August, forty-seven. The mountain routinely receives snowfall all months of the year.

The message did not strike home until we approached the summit of Mount Washington and encountered a series of weathered, wooden crosses wedged into the rocks. The crosses, we learned, marked the spots where hikers had died of exposure. One of the crosses, less than a quarter-mile from the summit house, served as a stark memorial to two hikers who had perished in a blizzard on July 18, 1958.

In the summit house, a list hangs from one wall with the names of the mountain's victims. Since 1849, more than one hundred people have died of exposure on Mount Washington, nearly a quarter of them during the summer. Often their bodies were recovered only a few hundred yards from shelter. The scenario is often the same: Fog materializes from nowhere or a sudden snowy whiteout descends, and visibility vanishes in minutes. Hikers clad in shorts and T-shirts, who might have been basking in warm sunlight only minutes earlier, suddenly find themselves drenched, shrouded in fog or snow, and buffeted by fifty- or sixty-mile-per-hour winds—the perfect recipe for hypothermia. The limited visibility leads to disorientation; the indistinct trails—snaking across boulder fields—disappear; and hikers stumble in circles. Soon, their body temperatures plunge below critical levels, their mental faculties dim, and they lie down in the snow and yield to death.

HERE THERE IS DEATH, THERE ARE TALES OF GHOSTS, and the Whites are no exception. Since 1979, I've returned to the Whites six times, and, while on a magazine assignment there in 1987, I had what remains my only paranormal experience. I was working on a story about the high-elevation huts of the area and was on the trail with Charlie, a college-aged hut keeper who had spent the preceding summer working in Lakes of the Clouds hut. For the better part of a week, Charlie and I traced the Appalachian Trail through the region, stopping each evening at a different hut.

One evening, we arrived at Mizpah Spring Hut, six miles south of Mount Washington, just before dusk. After the evening meal, as darkness descended, Charlie and I sat with the few dozen guests in the hut reading and talking in the golden glow of propane lamps. At 8:30 p.m., the hut keepers extinguished the lamps, and we navigated our way to our bunk rooms with flashlights. Though ours was ample to sleep a dozen hikers, Charlie and I were the room's only occupants.

Soon after we climbed into our bunks, the mountain sounds became amplified in the darkness. As the wind surged against the sides of the hut, every sash whined, and every rafter creaked and moaned. At the same time, I heard the distinct sound of some-one—or some thing—pacing across the floor above us. I didn't know it at the time, but the storeroom was directly above us. With its steeply pitched roof and large stores of flour sacks and other dry goods, it was unlikely that anyone could have navigated across the floor, much less stood upright while doing so.

The footsteps continued. A rhythmic, light step moving from one edge of the ceiling to the other, turning and pacing back. I asked Charlie, who had spent several summers working in the Whites, if he had any notion of what it was.

"Mice?" he ventured, as perplexed as I.

"Uh-uh," I said. "If that's mice, they're damned big mice, and they're wearing shoes."

"What else could it be?" he asked, after pausing to listen for a few seconds.

We drifted off to sleep to the sound of the incessant pacing.

At about 3:00 a.m., I had a dream. I call it a dream because I don't know what other term I could apply to it, but it was different from most dreams in that I experienced it in the semiconscious stage between sleep and wakefulness. It seemed too vivid to have been a dream.

It was night, and I was alone in an old, abandoned house ascending a long stairway. At the top, I arrived at a door that was ajar, and I pushed it open. Inside, the windowless room was dusky, not completely dark. There was no furniture on the scarred, wooden floor, and, on the right, I spotted a brick fireplace smudged with soot. A rusted flour tin rested on the hearth, and, as I spied it, it began to move, scraping in slow circles as if moved by an invisible hand.

As it moved, something across the room caught my attention. I peered to the left, across the floor toward an alcove at the far end of the room, and there I saw a shaft of gray light, like a translucent form, stretching from floor to ceiling. As I watched, it glided back and forth, tracing the width of the alcove. Though it had no shape—no discernible form, no features—I felt a strong presence in the room. Somehow I knew—I just knew—it was a woman, a young woman. A tingle surged up my spine, and I felt my hair stand on end as if I had just passed into a strong electrical current.

That's when I awoke and called to my friend, who slumbered in the bunk across the room.

"Hey, Charlie, I just saw a ghost!"

"Huh? You saw what?"

"I'm telling you, man, I just saw the ghost of a woman!"

"Are you sure it was a woman?"

"Absolutely!"

"Wow." Charlie said. "Listen, in the morning, tell the hut crew about this."

"Why?" I asked.

"I'd rather not say, but just do it."

The next morning, I recounted my experience to Mark, a hut-keeper at Mizpah in his early twenties. After I had finished, he calmly explained that, over the summer, dozens of other hikers had reported the same experience: first the footsteps, then the ghost. "Her name is Betsy," he said.

Betsy, he explained, was a young hiker who had drowned in a rain-swollen stream years earlier. The hut keepers had found her body near the hut. Because they were unable to transport the corpse down the mountain in the dark, they wrapped her in a sheet and placed it in the hut basement overnight.

"A short time later," Mark said, "people began to complain about the ghost."

The Kennebec River

Paul, Dan, and I forded the Kennebec River today, and I have never experienced a more sustained or intense rush in my life. When I reached the northern side, I lay in the grass quaking for the better part of a half-hour, feeling exhausted and exhilarated at the same time. The exhaustion soon passed, but the sense of accomplishment has remained with me through the day, and I suspect I'll carry it with me for months to come.

We had timed our crossing badly, as the dam upstream had already released its load, and, when we reached the bank, the rapids churned and roiled. As we prepared to plunge in, my resolve began to waver, particularly when I watched some of the other hikers in our group climb into a ferryman's boat for a risk-free ride to the other side. As I watched the boat leave the shore, I realized that I was committed, and the reality of what I was about to do scared me senseless.

I'd been contemplating this day for hundreds of miles, wondering if I'd have the guts to follow through. The crossing was as difficult—more difficult, in fact—than I had imagined, but in a similar way my strength and concentration exceeded my expectations, too.

SEPTEMBER 16, 1979
ABANDONED BARN NEAR MOXIE POND, MAINE

The Kennebec River, which sluices south through the center of Maine toward the Atlantic Coast, cost me more adrenalin, and, once I had crossed it, left me with a greater sense of accomplishment than any other stretch along the trail. Since then, it has served as the yardstick by which I measure the extremes of fear and exhilaration.

After feasting on an all-you-can-eat pancake breakfast at the Carrying Place, a backwoods pancake house, we eased north to the banks of the Kennebec at 8:00 a.m. on September 16.

The Kennebec represented an important emotional passage for me, and it allowed me to measure the courage I had gained over my months on the trail. Back in Georgia, I had been frightened by chipmunks rattling the underbrush. At that time, the notion of fording the Kennebec seemed foolhardy and dangerous, and I probably would have walked an additional 2,100 miles just to avoid it. But, by the time I reached Maine, my self-confidence had soared, and the Kennebec loomed more as a challenge than as an invitation for disaster. I realized, too, that facing the Kennebec would put my triumph over fear into a tangible perspective.

Positioned below a dam that releases thousands of tons of water each morning, the river crossing is known for its unpredictable conditions. At times, it is nothing more than a shallow ford that laps at the shins. At other times, it rages, exposing hikers to a belt-deep channel of torrid rapids.

When we reached the river, we realized that our timing was unfortunate. The dam had released its load, and the 150-foot-wide span of water was alive with riffles and eddies.

Paul, Dan, and I eyed the river and located a ragged line of riffles breaking on the surface, which marked the shallowest crossing. The shallowest stretch, we realized, also marked the fastest water. We clustered on the bank in the weeds for fifteen minutes or more, reviewing our strategy and donning our fording gear. Because the riverbed was strewn with rocks and boulders, we decided to leave our boots on. To attempt the ford in bare feet would leave our flesh tattered by the jagged rocks. There was another consideration, too. The current was so swift that, without the added support provided by the boots, if a foot had wedged between submerged boulders, ankle or shin bones would have snapped like green twigs, leaving us crippled and submerged.

There also was the question of traction. Along the trail, we had all careened into the weeds when our Vibram soles had glanced off damp rocks, and we knew that wet Vibram on wet, silt-covered stones would have provided us no purchase at all, never mind the tug of the current. So, we opted to pull on a pair of rag wool socks over our boots. The wool, similar to the felt worn by fishermen on the soles of their waders, would provide at least some grab.

Next, each of us foraged through the brush for an additional walking stick to supplement the one we already carried. The notion was to form a tripod, with the anchored foot as one base, and the stick in either hand as the second and third. That way, there would always be three points in contact with the bottom, and, if we happened to totter, we would have a chance to arrest our fall using one or both sticks.

Then, each of us unhooked his pack waistbelt. Over the years, the Kennebec has felled more than a few hikers. Those who were fortunate surrendered their packs to the current and reached shore drenched and shaken, but alive.

If our waistbelts had remained secured and we had taken a spill, the outcome would most certainly have been grim. The combined effect of the current, the unwieldy burden of a loaded pack, and the panic of being awash in a raging river would have left little hope of escape. With the belt unfixed, we stood a much better chance of jettisoning our packs if we submerged.

I chose not to dwell on those possibilities. In fact, I tried very hard not to think at all. If I had, I certainly would have pursued the sensible, risk-free means of crossing the river available to us at the time: As the three of us stood on the brink, a local boatman loaded several of our colleagues into his dinghy. For a few dollars, he would carry them safely across. Since 1985, when a woman drowned while fording the Kennebec, the Appalachian Trail Conference has admonished hikers to ferry across—the official route—rather than ford, and the organization, in concert with the Maine Appalachian Trail Club, now subsidizes a ferry service through the summer months.

"Woooow shit, Brill," shouted Dillon. "Do we really want to do this?"

"Just think about how great it will feel to get to the other side," I answered, as much to bolster my own failing confidence as to convince Paul of my commitment.

"Who's going first?" Paul asked. But, even as we stood quaking on the shoreline, his question had already been answered.

Dan was twenty yards away from the bank and sinking up to his pack straps in rapids. As we watched, I noticed that, for the first time since I had known him, his motion had lost its grace. I could see that he was straining against the current, fighting it with everything he had. On his upstream side, the water curled like a hydraulic battering ram where it struck his body.

As Dan reached the halfway point, Paul stepped into the water, and I watched the water lap farther and farther up his thighs and finally reach near his waist. Then, I knew that my moment of reckoning had come.

Paul and Dan were both endowed with long legs, while I am of a rather squat construction. My legs are strong, but they are also short. While the water reached just below Dan's and Paul's waists, it would reach to the middle of my own when I stepped into the deepest point.

As soon as I stepped in, I confronted an added hazard, one I hadn't anticipated. As I glanced at the rocks on the bottom through the rushing water, they seemed to waver, and, within a few feet, I began to suffer the effects of vertigo.

I realized, too, that I had vastly underestimated the force of the current. It felt as if the combined force of all those millions of tons of water was pinioned against my thighs, threatening to pull me down, pull me under.

I soon lost perception of time and space. Was I moving? The distant shore didn't look any closer, but the water had gotten progressively deeper. Yes, I must be moving, yet progress was so slow, measured in inches. Lift the upstream—the left-hand—walking stick. Force it into the current. Plant it. Lift the left foot. Keep the thigh and knee stiff against the current. Advance it several inches. Ease the muscles enough to allow the boot sole to bounce along the bottom until it wedged against a rock. Plant it. Lift the right stick. Plant. Lift the right leg. Plant.

Soon, a remarkable thing happened, something that I have experienced neither before nor since: I became so thoroughly focused on my task that motion seemed to cease, and I became lost in such complete concentration that the surrounding woods disappeared and the roar of the rapids faded. There were only the water, the rocks, the current, and I, fighting against all of them. There was the feeling that, if one muscle twitched, if the wind buffeted one strand of my hair, I would lose it. And, there was the feeling, too, that there would be a release in surrendering, in letting go the fight and yielding to the current.

As I reached the halfway point, I heard voices and whistling coming from the northern bank, and I glanced up. Paul and Dan stood on the bank waving frantically toward my right, downstream. It seems that I focused too intently on the riverbed and had strayed upstream into deeper water. Now, I faced the added burden of adjusting my course while continuing the ford.

Above the thunder of the water, I could hear my heart pounding in my ears. At the same time, I could feel surge after surge of adrenaline sparking my muscles.

Finally, the water began to inch down my stomach, then down my waist, my thighs, my knees. And I was safely across.

As I collapsed on the bank, the three of us recounted each step of the crossing like comrades who had survived the same battle. In many ways, it was a battle—a battle against current, rocks, vertigo, and fear. I had just experienced a rush so intense, so sustained, that, for a few minutes afterward, my muscles refused to respond at all; they only twitched.

As I lay on the bank, I began to understand the addictive power of risk. I could fathom why skydivers, high-elevation mountaineers, race-car drivers—people whose relative risk was much greater than what I had faced—willingly laid their lives on the line. Yes, the experience had been frightening. But, somehow, the mental clarity I had experienced during the crossing overrode the fear, and a sense of peace and security settled over me when I finally reached the northern bank of the Kennebec.

Katahdin

Climbing Katahdin didn't produce the emotional catharsis I had expected it would. Instead, the climb was like the last frantic dash to touch home plate. With each step, my anticipation of triumph grew, but, when I finally reached the summit, I felt a surge of sadness at realizing what I was about to leave behind. All of it: the rain, the cold, the mornings and evenings, the ascents and descents, the peaks, the friends, the seasons, the plants and animals, and the intimacy I've come to know with this world. I thought, too, about those things that I had already left behind. The continuum of my life has been broken. There are the events that occurred before the trail; then there is the trail. Those events seem thoroughly disjointed, as if from different lifetimes. The me of five months ago is a stranger. I am changed—forever.

SEPTEMBER 27, 1979
MOUNT KATAHDIN, MAINE

I caught my first, full broadside glimpse of Katahdin from the shore of Rainbow Lake Pond, twenty-seven miles and two days south of the trail's northern terminus. The sun shimmered off the fall foliage, and I could see where the ruff of red sugar maples and yellow birches yielded to scree and rock at the timberline. Katahdin, was and is, the most beautiful mountain I've ever seen, so perfect in shape and so solitary amid the sweep of flatlands.

As I viewed the mountain, I wanted to stop, to settle in and spend days or even weeks thinking about what those final few days meant. At the same time, there was an irresistible urge to confront the mountain, to trace its boulder-strewn shoulders, to reach its rounded, mile-high crown, and to complete the final leg of my journey. Katahdin had been the image in my sights for five months, especially in the early days when the peak seemed so distant and remote that we had little hope of reaching it. But, when I actually beheld the mountain, I knew I would finish and realized that my days on the trail were coming to an end.

On September 26, we reached the twin shelters at Katahdin Stream Campground. By that point, our ranks had swelled to nearly fifteen. Over the previous weeks, we had left entries in trail registers, urging our fellow thru-hikers to adjust their mileage so that we could make our summit bid *en masse*. Among those who joined our foursome were the Phillips brothers from Florida, Kansas native Jeff Hammons, newlyweds Phil and Cindy (who had honeymooned on the trail), North Carolina native Gary Owen, Jim Shaffrick from Connecticut, and Victor Hoyt, the Massachusetts hiker who had departed the trail in North Carolina.

We awoke on the morning of September 27 to clear blue skies. As we departed the shelters, the temperature hovered just above freezing.

The ascent to the summit of Katahdin is one of the stiffest along the entire trail: four thousand feet in just more than five miles. In places, the ascent requires hand-over-hand scrambling along rocky pitches, and, in other places, iron bars protrude from the rock and provide the only secure hand-holds.

But, I think I speak for most northbounders when I say that the difficulty of the ascent is negated by the sheer excitement of reaching the end of the trail. There were other factors as well that eased the strain of the ascent. For one thing, we were all in top physical form, having logged 2,100 miles of stiff ascents over the previous months. For another, before reaching the base of Katahdin, we had ambled through the rolling Lake Country without facing a major ascent for more than seventy miles, and our disdain for constant ascending and descending had passed. Our loads were much lighter than what we had become accustomed to, and we had supplanted our expedition packs with day packs, since we would be following the same route to the summit and back down to Katahdin Stream Campground. Then, there was the beauty of a perfect fall day. At every turn, autumn colors blazed, and, as we emerged above timberline at three thousand feet, every foot of elevation gained brought new vistas of the surrounding sphagnum bogs and shimmering lakes that captured parcels of the azure sky on their surfaces.

Despite the beautiful surroundings, I soon found myself so thoroughly absorbed in a tangle of conflicting emotions that I felt as though I were climbing alone, when, in fact, I was surrounded by companions. To reach the summit, I realized, would mean that I had achieved the goal, but then it occurred to me that I had already achieved other, more important goals over all the miles that had led me there. Katahdin was a formality—a definitive end point.

Once we reached the rock cairn that marked the top, Dan and I embraced. We surveyed the vast, flat Lake Country that sprawled for miles away from the mountain's base, and we studied the blue pockets of water fringed by acres of red and gold. Then, we sat peering silently toward the south, back across five months and 2,100 miles to Springer Mountain. There were so many things to say, yet none of them could be articulated.

If the white blazes had led farther north, I'm certain that all of us would have followed them. But they didn't. We had reached the end of the trail. It was time to leave the wilderness and return home.

CHAPTER FOURTEEN

Coming Home

We've reached the end of the trail, and we're heading back home to people and things that once were so familiar. Yet, I'm a bit apprehensive about how I'll respond to them and how they will respond to me. Will this experience make sense to anyone? Will things at home seem changed? Will I re-adjust? Will I remember all that I've seen, felt, learned, and shared over the past five months? Will I, in time, lose my intimacy with nature and begin to feel like a stranger when I visit the wilderness?

Tonight, there are fourteen of us gathered in adjoining hotel rooms in Millinocket celebrating the completion of our trek. Tomorrow, I say good-bye to friends whom I've come to know and love so well. Then, I will pile into a car for the trip home. The adventure continues.

SEPTEMBER 27, 1979
HOTEL ROOM, MILLINOCKET, MAINE

OUNT KATAHDIN REPRESENTED THE ONLY PEAK along the Appalachian Trail that proved more difficult to descend than ascend, yet that difficulty had nothing to do with terrain. For me, the 2,100 miles from Springer Mountain north had represented an unbroken continuum, a journey along a ridgeline corridor that was neatly contained between woodland walls and the southern and northern endposts. As long as I remained within those boundaries, my foremost designation was that of Appalachian Trail hiker, and my primary goal remained to reach the trail's northern terminus.

Once I had reached Baxter Peak, I realized that my next footfall would stray outside those boundaries and would lead inexorably away from the trail and away from the white blazes that for 150 days had provided all the direction I needed. The next step would lead away from a world of simple routine, away from a world governed by weather and shifting winds, where sun and seasons were the only time-keepers and where the measure of a day was in miles passed and insight gained. For the first time in more than five months, my path into the future was unclear.

As I reached the base of Katahdin, I confronted a tangle of conflicting emotions. I was proud of what I had accomplished, but I wondered what place my trail experiences would occupy in my life in the years that followed. I wondered if the lessons I had learned would be of use to me back home, and I wondered what I would do if I discovered that my new values clashed with those of civilized society. Would I have the courage to set off in my own direction? It would take me years to find the answers to those questions.

As daunting as the transition had been back in April, when, as a neophyte woodsman, I had struggled for security in a foreign environment, I suspected the transition back would be more difficult still. And more abrupt.

Twenty-four hours after reaching the summit of Katahdin, I had said a painful good-bye to my trail friends and was sitting in the passenger seat of a car cruising south along Interstate 95. As the car accelerated, I gripped the dashboard with white knuckles. Was it necessary to travel so fast, I asked the driver, a friend of Dan's who had agreed to shuttle us from Maine back home to Washington, D.C. He laughed and pointed to the speedometer. We were moving at fifty-eight miles per hour, yet, compared with the three-mile-an-hour pace I had maintained along the trail, it seemed as though we had broken the sound barrier.

Once we were out of Maine and away from the mountains and the accommodating residents of the trail towns, the people we encountered during our rest stops seemed to regard Dan and me, with our long beards and shabby clothes, as drifters or vagrants. Shopkeepers were abrupt, sometimes even rude. Diners at nearby tables glanced in our direction and muttered among themselves. As I confronted more and more suspicious faces, the pride that had evolved over the previous months began to ebb, replaced by self-consciousness and a feeling of being out of place. These people were clean and well-dressed. I was filthy. After several consecutive showers, I began to notice my pack and clothes reeked of sweat and campfire smoke. While these people abided by rules of etiquette, I attacked my food like a famished savage. As we exited a fast-food restaurant in Pennsylvania, I recall joking to Dan, "Well, Toto, I don't think we're in Kansas anymore." It occurred to me then that, if, after leaving the trail, I had strayed into a fairytale world peopled by dwarfs and witches, it wouldn't have seemed more skewed than this vision of mainstream America.

After a week back in Washington, the transition continued as I trimmed my beard, shed my trail clothes, and slipped into a navy-blue suit to be best man in a friend's wedding. Because I was penniless, the week after that, I sought work through a temporary employment service. On my first assignment, I spent four interminable days working as a file clerk and general lackey at a small corporate office. When a middle-aged woman chided me for misfiling a document, I wanted to explain to her that, after five months in the wilderness, the disposition of a file didn't seem all that vital to me, but I didn't. Instead, I resigned myself to the fact that, to the woman, my trail experiences were somewhat trivial, while my ability to alphabetize files was of paramount importance.

Two weeks after that, I returned home to Cincinnati and moved in with my parents. Though they had been supportive of my trail quest, they soon began to query me about my plans for the future. As it turned out, they weren't asking me anything that I hadn't been asking myself.

What followed was a slow, sometimes painful process of reentry marked by incidents that, taken together, made me wonder if my trek had been a tangential journey into the darkness rather than a pilgrimage toward self-discovery.

In October, I attended a party with some friends. By then, I had upgraded my wardrobe, and, although, in the sartorial sense, I fitted in with the rest of the partygoers, my attitudes and theirs seemed at odds.

"What have you been up to?" asked a friend whom I had not seen for several years.

"Well, I've spent the past five months in the woods, hiking the Appalachian Trail," I said, somewhat tentatively.

"Oh, is that right?" he responded. "My wife and I spent ten days in Europe this past summer."

He detailed his trip, then described his job as a sales representative for a large corporation. He told me how well he was doing and asked if I had noticed his new car parked out in front. I hadn't. He insisted on leading me outside to show it to me.

Afterward, he returned to the party while I settled into a rocking chair on the front porch. It was a cool October night, and I found relief in the breeze rustling the fallen leaves, the crisp smell of fall, and the stars—the same stars that had adorned night skies while I passed through fourteen states. But, beyond the glow of city lights, they seemed to have lost much of their luster, and I found myself wondering if my trail buddies had encountered the same difficulties. I wanted desperately to be with them. I knew Dan had abandoned his corporate career and had returned to Hot Springs. There, at the Inn, in the shadow of the mountains and surrounded by men and women who shared his trail values, he became an apprentice to a harpsichord builder. I regretted not having followed him there.

A couple of weeks, later I shaved my beard and, clad in dress clothes, set out to find a job. A career counselor who helped me prepare a résumé advised me not to include any mention of the Appalachian Trail among my accomplishments. He even suggested that I try to cover the gap it had created in my employment history.

"No one will see much value in your hiking experiences," he said. "They will only see that you were unemployed for those months."

I bristled at his suggestion that I should hide my adventure between lines on a résumé or, worse, twist it into a nonevent, something that I should deny ever happened.

Despite his advice, I did include the trail on my résumé, and it has appeared on every résumé I've drafted since. I eventually landed a job in a backpacking shop, and, though the position didn't pay much, it kept me in touch with people who, like me, lived for weekend forays into the woods.

During my tenure at the backpacking shop, in my years as a writer, and in all the relationships and roles that have occupied my life since 1979, I have drawn on my experiences from the trail. Though it took a while to realize it, the trail had shaped me, had given me a philosophy, had toughened me in some ways, had softened me in others, and had taught me lessons I will never forget: lessons on survival, kindness, strength, friendship, courage, perseverance, and the ways of nature. Those lessons have affected everything I've done since.

From weeks of living out of a thirty-five-pound pack, I learned to find contentment in simple things and to rely on myself and my resources to surmount obstacles. From long days spent tromping through rain and cold, I learned that, whenever I felt beaten, spent, exhausted, and ready to quit, there was always something left, and if I delved deep enough, I could always find the strength to keep moving forward. From watching the seasons yield one to the next, daylight surrender to night, and darkness give way to morning, I discovered that, in the midst of chaos, order and purpose are present for us. From the unqualified kindness shared among travelers in the back country, I learned that, for all the cruelty loose in the world, most people care deeply for their fellow creatures. And, I learned that, whenever I lose sight of those lessons, I can regain them by returning to the trail.

In the spring of 1987, I left my job as an editor with a large southeastern publishing company—a job that never really felt right for me—to pursue a full-time career as a free-lance writer. The transition was not as graceful as I had hoped, and I passed months of despondency when the assignments I sought didn't come. I decided to quit, but, before I did, I loaded my pack and set out for Springer Mountain. The trail had answered my needs once before, and I had faith that it would do so again. Over the following weeks, I mingled with the new class of thru-hikers and formed new, lasting friendships as I ambled along flower-speckled trails and savored the verdant arrival of spring. I also discovered that, though the circumstances of my life had changed, the trail had remained the same—just as charged with life and hope as I remembered it. A month after I began, and 335 miles farther north, I was healed and returned to my chosen occupation more determined than ever. In time, I succeeded.

INCE 1937, THOUSANDS OF SEEKERS HAVE COURSED along the trail's miles, each pursuing a personal mission, each in search of something enduring and real. Among those hikers I came to know there was Elizabeth, who took up the trail seeking relief from the grief of losing her husband. There was Nick, who forged a new direction for his life after retirement. As for Paul, Dan, and the rest of us, fresh from college, we set out to learn the lessons of the wilderness before we learned the lessons of the professional world, and, somewhere along the way, we all found what we were looking for. The answers may not have been exactly what we sought, but I believe they were precisely what we needed.

I suspect that the trail will continue to work its magic on the hundreds of future end-to-enders who in years hence will arrive at Springer, sign the log book, and point their boots and hopes north. I suspect, too, that, years and years from now, after we have followed our new technologies and grand urban schemes into a new century, the trail will remain a sure route into our past, a route along which technology will always surrender to strength and spirit and the laws of nature.

VER THE PAST TWENTY-FIVE YEARS, MY MEMORIES OF THE months on the trail have survived as a time of sublime happiness, a time when I felt my neurons being switched on for the very first time. The mention of the trail still evokes images of lush, green mountains; of great, gray clouds of mist wafting through virgin stands of hemlock and oak; of bald-topped mountains with views that roll out as far as the eye can see, across miles and miles of blue-hazed hills; of hawks swirling above sun-drenched granite ledges; of springs that ran so cold they made my teeth ache.

My other memories also grow more vivid and precious with time. No matter how many times I have hefted my backpack, picked up the white blazes, and trod my favorite sections of the trail, the excitement—the sense of discovery—has never failed me. I doubt that any other event of my life will choke me with as much emotion, fill me with as much pride, or define more clearly who I am than my summer on the Appalachian Trail.

CHAPTER FIFTEEN

Appalachian Reunion: Twenty Years Later

Reprinted with permission from National Geographic Traveler.

RUMMHOLZ," SAYS VICTOR HOYT, PAUSING JUST long enough to give the word the appropriate emphasis. He gestures with a ski pole toward a diminutive, wind-twisted balsam fir that has somehow managed to root itself into the triangle of black soil wedged between giant rocks.

"Krummholz means we're about to hit tree line," he shouts over his shoulder, and I'm vaguely aware that the canopy of red maple and yellow birch has given way to a widening patch of blue sky.

Victor is a compact man with the stout thighs and lean upper body of an alpinist. Graying curls emerge from a yellow bandanna tied pirate style, and his ski poles clack rhythmically on granite boulders the size of church buses. He advances up the slope and shrinks in perspective as he pulls away from me. I follow, scrambling over rocks, wedging my boots into cracks, gripping the edges of lichen-covered stone, and hauling myself and my backpack up and over exposed ledges. Eventually I stumble onto a tight patch of flat ground outlined by huge boulders.

"See, I knew we were close to tree line," Victor says, pointing behind me. "Look."

I turn, and suddenly my perspective explodes, extending for miles unbroken across the vast lake country of central Maine. The terrain plunges away 2,000 feet beneath us. Some 1,700 feet above lies our destination, Baxter Peak, high on the summit ridge of Mount Katahdin, where the white paint blazes marking the Appalachian Trail abruptly end.

For Victor and me, and the four other hikers in our party laboring up below us—Dan Howe, Paul Dillon, Jimmy Black, and Nick Gelesko—Baxter Peak is where we'll have a mile-high homecoming. We've converged from Washington, Massachusetts, North Carolina, Tennessee, Florida, and the Bahamas to hike the final thirty-five miles of the A.T. and to stand atop Katahdin twenty years from the day since we gathered here in 1979.

Back in 1979, Dan and I started the trek after meeting by chance in Reston, Virginia, and we picked up the others along the way. Back then, I was twenty-three, lean, bearded, clad in threadbare clothes, and poised to begin my life. Back then, with the exception of Nick, we were just kids. Now we're grown-ups. And in the years since we first did the trail, the six of us have produced eighteen kids, seventeen grandkids, seven great grand-kids, eight marriages, and four divorces. And we've pursued careers as wide-ranging as broncobuster, greens-keeper, and rock musician. Today, Victor is an organ builder in Northhampton, Massachusetts. Dan is a Raleigh, North Carolina, city planner. Paul carpenters in Seattle. Jimmy is an elephant management consultant at the Atlanta Zoo. I'm a writer living in the Tennessee woods. And Nick?

Age 57 back in '79, he's now retired and living with his wife, Gwen, in Florida. He is beginning to show his age, having advanced into the final column on the actuarial tables. A raw incision runs from ear to collar on his neck, a souvenir of a recent emergency procedure to repair a clogged carotid artery (he had survived two earlier bypass surgeries). He is at the upper age limit for Appalachian Trail hikers, and eight weeks of recovery hardly seems adequate for the five-day trek we face. It's a given that the 4,000-foot ascent to Katahdin's summit will tax him. It grinds down young men and women who've been training for almost 2,200 miles. We just hope it doesn't kill him.

HAD JUST DROPPED OUR CAR OFF AT THE TAKE-OUT point and was heading to meet my companions who had gone on ahead. The bite of spruce hung in the air, and my backpack—groaning with food and supplies—settled onto my hips and tugged at my shoulders, familiar, comforting. My mind, drifting back twenty years, swam with memories: Of the profile of 6,288-foot Mount Washington, New England's tallest peak, 118 trail miles distant in the White Mountains of New Hampshire. Of traversing mile-long Mahoosuc Notch, an obstacle course of house-sized boulders that required us to crawl on hands and knees and squeeze, dragging our packs, through tight fissures in the rocks. Of being pummeled by Hurricane David's cold rains as we meandered through spruce forests so intensely green that you could almost watch the nitrogen cycle at work. How thirty miles from the nearest road, in the ancient fishing cabin at Antler Camp on the shores of Jo-Mary Lake, we harvested freshwater mussels and lake trout (later, we fried them up in butter, feasted into the night, then lay on our backs watching meteors streak across a black night sky).

In what seemed like an instant, I heard the murmur of voices and saw the glow of a campfire ahead through the trees. As I slid from my pack, I realized that, despite the crow's feet and paunches, little had changed since we had last gathered around a campfire.

Nick, having whipped up a batch of his trademark pudding, lounged on a foam sleeping mat in the same outfit he had sported in 1979—khaki shirt adorned with trail patches, trousers bound at the waist by rope, and stout, 1970s-era hiking boots. Victor stirred a pot of sautéing vegetables. Paul, at forty-one the youngest in our group, sat on a chair-size cube of granite and hugged his knees to his chest. His face had aged little, though gray now streaked the dense thicket of hair that obscured the collar of his fleece jacket. Dan, forever in motion, circled the fire and poked the coals, triggering a geyser of rising sparks. Absent his white canvas hat, checkered wool shirt, and ample beard, he looked like a Republican version of his former Woodstock-era self, but the voice, full of music and energy, was the same. And, there was Jimmy, pulling a bottle of mango rum from the side pocket of his pack and asking: "Anyone care to sample a bit of Bahamian sunshine?"

HE NEXT MORNING, VICTOR, WHO SEEMED TO REGARD sleep as a necessary evil, stood leaning on ski poles, pack straps cinched tight, eager to get moving. The rest of us elected to linger over coffee before we headed out. We caught up with him at Rainbow Stream Lean-to.

Many of the current class of thru-hikers had left their mark in the spiral-bound register that contained the musings of Blisters, Disco, Hyper, Repartee, Triscuit, Greenfood, Slyfox, Charlie Hustle, Bear Paw, Grizzly, Rainbow Bright.

By midafternoon, we reached the rocky shores of Rainbow Lake, one of dozens of pockets of blue water that dot the lowlands of central Maine. I pieced together my fly rod and waded to my waist, eager to see if my angling skills had evolved since my first passage through these parts, when I was armed with a $12 telescoping rod-reel outfit from K-Mart. As the chill water lapped my thighs, thickening wisps of cirrus clouds, tinged pink and deep purple, caught the last rays of sun.

Lifting the line off the water, I false-casted until I'd stripped out thirty feet and dropped a caddisfly into the concentric rings that signaled a rising fish. In an instant, a trout broke the surface, and I felt the line go tight. Twenty years ago, I might have regarded the fish as supplemental protein, but tonight I released him as I smelled garlic and fresh basil sautéing back in camp. Later, clad in fleece pants and pullovers, the six of us sat with plates empty and bellies full—and the stories tumbled out ....

About the day in New Hampshire when Dan, spotted with twenty-six welts inflicted by a swarm of yellow jackets, retrieved his walking stick from within two feet of the nest. About the cold, rainy night in Rangeley, Maine, when Nick cajoled us lodging at the local jail when no one else would take us in. About the drunk in a Tennessee bar who waved a loaded gun in our faces. About the aggressive farm dogs that often confronted us, snarling, when we'd enter small towns along the route.

"Dogs are bad, but pigs are much worse," Paul said, colorfully relating an involved story of being chased by a large, territorial sow somewhere in the southern reaches of the trail.

"No, hippos are the worst," countered Jimmy, who spent three years guiding elephant safaris in Botswana. "I've had lions sleep five feet from my tent, and I've been chased by bull elephants, but nothing's as frightening as a hippo. They explode out of the water with mouths open wide, and, on land, they can run maybe 20 miles an hour." We conceded that Jimmy had the better-informed perspective.

HE NEXT MORNING, WE SCALED RAINBOW LEDGES— where clouds conspired to block our first view of Mount Katahdin—before descending to Hurd Brook Shelter, nestled in a dense fir and spruce forest. Then, we headed on to Abol Bridge Campground Store on Golden Road, a two-laner traveled mostly by loggers, hunters, and the fall-foliage fanatics known in these parts as leaf-peepers. This junk-food shrine is beloved by those to whom it marks the end of the longest stretch of unbroken forest (the so-called Hundred-Mile Wilderness). And, Linda Belmont, who bought the camp store in 1978, evoked our past when she produced a stack of dirt-smudged index cards bearing our 1979 sentiments and signatures.

From our campsite behind the store on the sandy shore of Abol Stream, we studied the southwestern face of Katahdin, looming fifteen miles and two trail days to the north. The colors on its steep slopes shifted from gold to red and finally to gray. Long after sunset, the mountain became a hulking shadow outlined by stars.

From Abol Bridge, we paralleled the Penobscot River, where, a century ago, spring freshets floated millions of tons of logs down to the sawmills in Bangor. Today, rafters, not logs, bounce over the river's gentle riffles. Then, we crossed into Baxter State Park, a 203,733-acre wilderness area, and began the big slog—gradual at first, then pitched—from 580 feet above sea level to Katahdin's mile-high summit. To the Wabanaki Indians, Ktaadn ("highest land") was the sacred home of the sometimes wrathful storm god, Pomola. Defying her in 1846, Henry David Thoreau scaled to within 500 feet of the summit before fog, cold, and howling winds forced him to retreat. "The tops of mountains are among the unfinished parts of the globe," wrote Thoreau in his book, *Ktaadn*. "Only daring and insolent men, perchance, go there.... Pomola is always angry with those who climb to the summit of Ktaadn."

Count the six of us among those "insolent men." And, forgive me for taking issue with Thoreau. Pomola is not always angry. In 1979, we reached Katahdin's summit on a cold, cloudless day. And when, on September 27, 1999, we arose before dawn at Katahdin Stream Campground for the assault on the mountain, we were greeted by a canopy of winking stars.

 UST AS I CINCHED THE DRAWSTRING TO MY PACK, I noticed Victor impatiently poking the ground with his ski poles. "Ah, if you guys don't mind, I think I'm going to start moseying," he said. This meant he would accelerate to a blistering pace maintained until he reached the highest ground.

"I'm coming with you," I replied, shouldering my pack and preparing to hitch my tow rope to Vic-of-the-massive-thighs.

"See you boys on top," I said.

Nick came over to wish me well.

"You know, I'm more excited about this climb than back in '79," he confessed. For the first time, I heard fear in his voice.

"I have a lot of anxiety about this," he continued. "A lot of anxiety."

"Nick, you can do this," I replied, but I remembered the hiker who yesterday had straggled down the mountain past me with hollow, exhausted eyes.

"Remember Nick, the ascent is optional," I said. "The descent is mandatory."

Soon, I was climbing. Sweat soaked the foundation layer of my fleece; the bandanna around my head started to drip. I fixed my gaze on the patch of trail directly in front of me and started to flow through the topography. Eventually, Victor's voice dragged me back.

"Krummholz," he said. "I love krummholz."

HEAD, STILL MORE THAN A MILE DISTANT, WE SEE tiny hiker forms moving up the gray summit ridge of Baxter Peak. And then, we're on top. It's 10:45 a.m., and we've covered the 5.2 miles in just over three hours. So far, there's no sign of Nick and the rest of our gang. Two hours pass. Temperatures climb into the high sixties. Another hour lapses.

"We should go down if they don't show soon," Victor says.

Finally, Jimmy arrives. He had left behind his expedition pack in favor of Dan's convert-a-pack that doubles as luggage. Near the summit, he extends the plastic handle and rolls his load the final few feet.

"Can anyone direct me to Gate 15?" he asks.

Then, Paul appears. Down on the Tableland, I see Nick picking his way up the slope. His motion is slow, halting, unsteady. It takes him forty minutes to cover the last 500 feet. But, finally, he arrives on the summit. And, his five colleagues spontaneously break into applause.

He stands ramrod straight, his black beret cocked. He smiles weakly, slowly drinks in the view, then reclines on granite.

"That was a bit harder than I remember it," he says.

"How are your legs, Nick?" I ask.

"Just fine as long as I stay in this position. But, it's damned good to be here."

We gather arm-in-arm for a summit picture. I'm emotional. So many memories converge here on this peak, and this mountain and this moment will, for the rest of my life, remain fused as one. We'll regroup in twenty years, we promise ourselves. But, the odds are that we will be five, not six. And, I am filled with sadness at the thought.

It was on the trail, in 1979, that I began to grasp that the end-less cycling of seasons—the perfect metaphor for life—is meant to bring us around, to guide us home. Which is why I returned to Maine, to gather with men who are, and always will be, part of my family and, for a time, to reduce the complexity of my life to the simplicity of a white blaze and a dirt path heading north.

CHAPTER SIXTEEN

A Passage, at Midlife, along the Smokies AT

ALL ME PANGLOSS.

C Back in the city, I'm known by my given name, but out here I assume a different identity. The budding hardwoods, the trilling warblers, and the spring beauties whose abundance suggests a late-season dusting of snow, are all markers of a forest in the throes of a magical seasonal transition. Like the forest, I am in transition, too.

I'm suffering from a repetitive motion injury—in this case, one that has settled in my brain. The ailment was triggered by nearly two decades in the same reasonably comfortable chair, contained within the same stark eggshell-white office walls, and producing a bourgeoning mountain of word-bearing pages, all in exchange for my monthly food pellet and access to affordable healthcare.

Dr. Pangloss, the irrepressible—and, many would argue, harle-quinesque—optimist from Voltaire's novella *Candide*, is the man I hope to become over the coming nine days, which will lead me 72 miles through Great Smoky Mountains National Park along the famed Appalachian Trail (AT)—a lofty path that most would agree is the most elegant vantage point from which to experience the Smokies.

This article first appeared in the spring 2009 edition (No. 4) of *Smokies Life* magazine. The magazine is published by Great Smoky Mountains Association. Phone: 1-888-898-9102. Web: http://smokiesinformation.org/

The realm I'm entering is, in my estimation, "the best of all possible worlds," as Pangloss would have termed it. Before I arrive at journey's end at Davenport Gap and I-40, I will have witnessed the bounteous and colorful arrival of spring and shared trail miles and gathered in camp with more than 40 fellow hikers. Many of them, like me, have adopted names more reflective of their aspirations than their genealogy.

I shed my city clothes, don my hiking togs and lug-soled boots, shoulder my backpack, and depart the cushy digs at Fontana Village just after dawn. As I do, I begin the mental and spiritual transformation from working stiff to AT hiker somewhere between the parking lot at the south end of Fontana Dam and the point a half mile beyond where the blacktop ends and the two-by-six-inch white blazes marking the 2,175-mile AT enter the park.

As I walk across the dam, rain dimples the surface of Fontana Lake, an impoundment created by the Tennessee Valley Authority in the 1940s. Low-slung clouds drape the greening spring forest, and their wispy tendrils caress the lake's surface, creating a primordial scene despite the millions of tons of poured concrete under foot.

The emotional transition to Pangloss will prove easier to achieve than the cumulative gain (and loss) of 18,500 feet in altitude that will lead me to summits of some of the highest peaks in the East by trip's end. From the lake, in just under four miles, I will gain 2,100 feet, bearing a 50-pound pack groaning with a six-day supply of food.

The profile of the AT through the park trends steadily upward for 33 miles from the dam, culminating atop Clingmans Dome, at 6,643 feet, the highest peak in the park as well as on the entire AT.

Mountains of Memory

'VE STOOD AT THIS THRESHOLD BEFORE, WITH MY BOOTS and my hopes pointed north and with a heart open to new experience. The first time, in the spring of 1979, I approached the southern threshold of the Smokies as a 23-year-old, fresh from college and with my AT odometer reading just under 200 miles. Fontana Lake greeted me then, as now, wearing a shroud of mist.

By summer's end, nearly 2,000 miles later, I would stand atop the AT's northern terminus, Mount Katahdin, and, for the first time in more than five months, seek a path through life that wasn't clearly marked by the AT's familiar white blazes.

The AT is the first and arguably the most famous U.S. National Scenic Trail and one of the longest continuously marked footpaths in the world, passing through 14 states, eight national forests, and six national park units, including the Smokies. Each year, about 4 million people pass miles on the AT, among them, more than a thousand aspiring thru-hikers, as they are called, who typically arrive at the trail's southern terminus, Springer Mountain, Georgia, and begin the long journey north.

By the time they reach Maine, in an average year, their ranks will have been thinned by 80 percent, owing to poor preparation, injury, or an irrepressible longing for creature comforts or forlorn lovers back home.

Those who complete the route arrive in Maine physically and spiritually transformed by the experience.

For me, the most marked effect was the evolution from someone who visited the wilderness to a person who regarded the woods as his home.

The Wages of Age and Gravity

T HE INTERVENING 29 YEARS HAVE, SADLY, ERODED THAT precious connection with the natural world and left me with 20 excess pounds and middle-aged knees that haven't borne the heft of a backpack for nearly eight years.

Those knees are talking to me as I toil up the steep, rocky trail toward 4,000-foot Mt. Shuckstack, whose fire tower offers some of the best views in the western portion of the park. I stop frequently to lean heavily on my trekking poles and breathe. The rain eases as I ascend, and I note that the canopy begins to open; the branches of the hardwoods above 4,000 feet are still largely barren. Beneath them, the forest floor displays an abundance of ferns and wildflowers, all basking in a few weeks of direct sunlight before the deciduous trees unfurl their leaves and cast the ground in lingering summer shade.

Spring beauties, trout lilies, white and crimson trilliums, and bluets abound at the zone of transition between winter and spring.

After nearly two hours, I arrive at the base of Shuckstack and encounter the first of my fellow wayfarers, sprawled out—along with items from their foodbags—at trailside on a relatively flat patch of ground. Daryl Holloway and John Morrison, college students from Florida, are out for a few days on the trail before beginning the summer term back at school.

Their plastic bag containing an orderly stack of tin cans tells me that they, like me, are catering to their stomachs at the expense of their thighs. Such decisions seem ill-advised on the steep ascents but fully justified once we're in camp and poised over simmering cook pots.

The thru-hikers would laugh at such extravagance, all the while salivating mightily at the sight of canned meats.

Several hundred yards ahead, I meet Daryl and John's colleague, Tyler Stock, sitting impatiently by the trail, wondering what's keeping his friends.

With the bulk of the day's climb behind me, I amble up and over a series of unremarkable knobs before arriving at Birch Springs Campsite, situated at 3,834 feet, a few hundred yards off the AT. A well-used fire ring and jumble of outsized logs abandoned by an overly ambitious campfire engineer mark the spot of the shelter that once stood here. Described by a friend on the park staff as a dank, malodorous hovel, the shelter was removed in 2000. Instead, the park has created a series of leveled tent platforms. A sign at the entrance to the camp provides directions to the spring, campsites, and, sufficiently distant and downstream, the latrine area.

Blessedly alone for the time, I scan the hills rising on both sides of the draw and can easily picture a bruin, newly emerged from his winter den, scouting for an easy meal. Over my many days and nights in the park, I have met five bears in the backcountry and in all cases savored the encounters and the elemental wildness of these remarkable creatures. All eyed me warily and made no effort to approach, suggesting that they had not been corrupted through their encounters with some of the ill-mannered animals who walk on two legs.

Since my last visit, the park staff has installed ingenious bear-deterrent devices at all shelters and campsites. A stout cable, 20 feet off the ground, spans two trees about 20 yards apart. A series of color-coded cables clips to eye bolts screwed into the trunk of one of the trees near the ground. The cables feature hooks for securing food bags or entire packs, which are then hoisted and dangle out of reach of marauding bears.

Large metal discs—picture enormous pie pans—attach to the cable near the anchors, preventing smaller critters from engaging in a desperate high-wire act to snatch food.

A Simple Shelter

OR THIS TRIP, I HAVE ESCHEWED THE WEIGHT OF A TENT since I will be slumbering in shelters for all but this first night. Instead, I pack a 6-by-8-foot plastic tarp, which I erect using my trekking poles and 50 feet of nylon cord.

After securing my shelter, I fill my plastic bladder with filtered water from the spring, slip into my warm fleece, and engage in what will become an afternoon ritual. Resting on my sleeping pad against a stout log below a hillside spread with wildflowers and with the afternoon sun emerging from the clouds, I set a pot of water to boil within easy reach and open a tattered copy of *Walden*— a companion on many of my backcountry forays.

The wrapper for my herbal tea bag admonishes me to "ease into that good feeling," and so I do, in the company of Henry David Thoreau, who articulates the sentiment in a slightly more eloquent way: "In any weather, at any hour of the day or night, I have been anxious to improve the nick of time, and notch it on my stick; to stand on the meeting of two eternities, the past and the future, which is precisely the present moment; to toe that line."

I heed Thoreau's advice and fully surrender to the present: a steaming pot of tea, a comfortable place to lounge, a sun-dappled spring forest, a simple shelter, and a backpack containing all the essentials of my life, at least for the time being.

Thru-hiker Dick MacPherson, a.k.a. Lion King (a nod to his affiliation with the Middletown, Massachusetts, Lions Club), arrives at the campsite early in the evening and joins me and the three college students from Florida. At 63, Lion King, a retired electrician, amateur bee keeper, and brew master, represents half of the latest demographic trend among thru-hikers. Back in 1979, I could have counted on one hand the number of fifty-plusers on the trail. There were also few women—much to the disappointment of us 23-year-old guys. By contrast, in nine days, by the time I reach Davenport Gap, half of the 46 hikers I meet will fall into the 50-plus age bracket, and more than a quarter of the 46 will be women.

Lion King, like most thru-hikers, is traveling light, which means he left his ponderous winter sleeping bag at home. I did the same, assuming that the warm, humid weather would hold through my trip. It doesn't. By 9:00 P.M., the temperature is hovering in the low-40s as I climb into my sleeping bag—a pancake-flat, 25-year-old synthetic-fill model once rated to 35 degrees. I can see stars winking beyond the edge of the tarp, but by midnight, the wind and rain begin to buffet the tarp, and I can feel the temperature plunge.

By morning, the tarp is glazed with ice, and ice crystals bob in my plastic water bottles. Lion King's thermometer recorded an overnight low of 22 degrees Fahrenheit. Farther north on the trail, and a thousand feet higher, those slumbering at the Spence Field Shelter experienced a couple of inches of snow and a low of 18 degrees.

The wildflowers, particularly the May apples, seem to have fared the worst. Their once lush green umbrellas are now drooping, flash-frozen victims of the sudden chill.

En route to Russell Field Shelter, my destination 8.6 miles north, I depart the camp by 10:00 A.M. in full sunshine, but I retain the fleece layers for warmth.

Within five miles, I arrive at Mollies Ridge Shelter at noon and meet Bill and Sharon Van Horn, a retired army officer and English teacher, respectively, from Franklin, North Carolina. The Van Horns are two of more than 30 "ridge runners" and caretakers positioned at high-use areas, like the Smokies, along the AT route. The ridge runner program is managed by the Appalachian Trail Conservancy (ATC), the nonprofit organization dedicated to the protection of the AT corridor.

Bill and Sharon are here to provide information and advise hikers on the rules of passage through this, the most visited national park in the country, and to minimize impacts to the natural environment.

In my memory, the shelters along the AT through the Smokies were dismal, cramped, mouse-infested structures furnished with chain-link enclosures to prevent bears from entering—in effect, zoos in reverse. Many of the Smokies AT shelters date to the Civilian Conservation Corps of the 1930s and '40s, and, frankly, by the late-1970s, they had begun to show signs of age and overuse.

Over the past several years, the National Park Service has been renovating one shelter per year in the Smokies, removing the fencing—made obsolete by the highly effective food-hanging cables—restoring sleeping platforms, repairing stonework, and in some cases, enlarging the shelter area, installing skylights, and constructing privies. Mollies Ridge is the first of the restored shelters I encounter, and the contrast with the shelters of my memory is remarkable. It's open, airy, and remarkably clean. And the bear cables seem to have eradicated—or at least significantly reduced—the population of foraging mice that once inhabited the shelters.

Back on the trail, just over an hour later, I approach Russell Field. The opening of the forest, pocket meadows of native grasses, and ancient, flowering fruit trees bear testament to the field's early use as summer pasture for the farm families inhabiting lands that would become the national park. When I arrive at the shelter, I'm initially disappointed to see the bear fencing intact—apparently, the restoration crew hasn't yet reached this shelter.

Here, 29 years ago, I experienced a crush of humanity. Nineteen hikers occupied the shelter, with a couple of canine souls thrown in, despite the park's strict policy barring dogs from the backcountry.

By late afternoon, Russell Field has become a bustling social hub, and it appears as though the crowd converging here will exceed shelter capacity. I meet Flip (Steve Rollins, 31), his partner Flop (Nikki Roberson, 31), and Nikki's father, Peppers (Jerry Roberson, 55). The threesome, from Bloomington, Indiana, is thru-hiking together.

Close behind them arrive Ohioan Waters (Kelly Collins, 23), Mainer Frumpy (Sean Thurston, 22), Floridian Day Hiker (Dan Sweeney, 63), Rhode Islanders Chef (Neath Pal, 45) and his brother-in-law Soupy (Tim Toolan, 40), and New York City CPA Pete's Draggin' (Peter Talluto, 32).

Over coming days, Day Hiker, Chef, Soupy, and Pete's Draggin' will become part of my trail family. On the AT, where the quality of the companionship seems to increase in proportion to the distance from the nearest road, friendships evolve quickly.

Each hiker has his or her own deeply personal reason for being out here. Chef, a Cambodian émigré who owned a successful French-Asian restaurant in Providence, sold the stressful enterprise so he could more fully enjoy his life and his two young children. He's section hiking the trail—doing a few weeks on the trail each year—with brother-in-law Soupy, an administrator at the University of Rhode Island.

Pete's hoping to climb through the window of opportunity that will close when he marries, buys a house, and starts a family. "I have no wife, no mortgage, no kids," he tells me. "I don't know how long that will last."

Peppers read an article on the AT in the Bloomington newspaper a decade ago, and once he retired from Frito-Lay, set out to fulfill a dream.

Day Hiker paraphrases Thoreau in explaining his quest: "Many people die without having lived."

Around dinner time, I get my first lessons on the ultra-light mindset of the contemporary thru-hiker. Day Hiker, like many of the hikers I meet on the trail, has fashioned his alcohol stove from two soda cans. The device weighs all of a couple of ounces. His weight shaving didn't stop there. He's carrying roller-ball pen refills—minus the plastic housing—to write in his journal. He is wearing shoes that seem better suited to running marathons than crunching rugged trail. His tiny titanium cook pot—wrapped in an insulating cozy to retain heat—is just large enough to hold his requisite calories for each meal.

He commandeered his wife's sewing machine to create a one-pound tent that doubles as a pillow. He also crafted a functional but odd-looking hat—crafted from silver rip-stop nylon and down—that might peg him as a medieval serf or a space alien.

Day Hiker studies my cooking rig—a one-liter fuel bottle connected to a white-gas stove supporting a four-quart pot, all shrouded by an aluminum windscreen.

"Man, you could feed a whole camp with that pot!" he observes. Then he hefts my pack. "Ugh!" is all he says, shaking his head reprovingly.

Searching for Bears—and Bars

LACK BEARS ARE TO THE SMOKIES WHAT MOOSE ARE TO Baxter State Park in Maine—iconic symbols and requisite viewing for anyone determined to experience these places fully.

Bears are a topic of conversation at each of the shelters I visit, but only three of the 40-some hikers I meet will actually glimpse one of them. In this case, myth and legend supplant reliable, first-hand information on the creatures.

Back in 1979, like many of the hikers I'm gathered with here at Russell Field, I operated under wildly erroneous information about bears. I regarded them as fearful and aggressive animals that would likely maul me to get at my food bag, and yet, I was eager to actually see one—provided from a safe distance. In preparation for just such an encounter, and in stark violation of park rules, I carried a string of firecrackers in my pack to use as a deterrent.

Today, after having seen several bears in the backcountry, all without incident, I'm amused by the ludicrous image of a terrified hiker, frantically shedding his pack, rummaging for the firecrackers, and lighting the fuses with trembling hands, all while an indifferent bear passively looks on.

Though bears are feared and respected, it's the invasive and populous wild hog that inspires the most fear. We've all seen evidence of the creatures' destructive excavation along the trail leading to the shelter. One hiker surmised that the upturned soil along the trail's margins meant that the Park Service was widening the footpath.

"A local guy a ways back told me that the hogs are docile if you encounter them during the day," says Pete's Draggin.' "But at night, it's a different matter. This guy told me that you *don't even want to know* what they'll do to you if you run into them after dark!"

The hikers ringed around Pete respond to his tale with sober grunts.

Rather than reach for a string of firecrackers, I suspect that the contemporary thru-hiker might, instead, reach for his cellular phone to summon help.

Despite their bent toward saving weight, nearly all thru-hikers I meet carry cell phones, which they recharge during stops in town. Those with personal digital assistants are able to access the Web and send emails from the heart of the wilderness.

In 1979, the highest-tech electronic devices in our packs were the simple flashlights we carried—the Casio digital watch was still lurking on the horizon, and the "why-didn't-we-think-of-this-sooner" hiker headlamp had yet to be commercialized.

Tomorrow morning, before we depart Russell Field Shelter, I will peer through the chain link and see a half-dozen hikers roaming about the grassy meadow, cell phones held aloft, endeavoring to muster sufficient bars to make a quick call home.

At one point, Pete's Draggin' will hand me his iPhone and ask me to snap a picture, which he subsequently will send as an email attachment to his girlfriend working in a high-rise office in New York City.

"She's having a bad day," he will say. "This ought to cheer her up."

Hiker Midnight

Y 8:00 P.M., AS THE SUNLIGHT BEGINS TO FADE, I NOTE a mass migration toward tents and berths in the shelter. Bill and Sharon, the ridge runners I met at Mollies Ridge Shelter, had remarked that "8 is hiker midnight." Indeed, by 8:30, we're all tucked into our bags. A few of us read by the light of our headlamps, but even those are extinguished by 9.

Earlier in the evening, Day Hiker made a point of asking me if I snored.

"Only if I have a cold or have swilled too much bourbon," I tell him. "And neither applies tonight."

I notice later that he has positioned his sleeping bag proximate to mine.

After a brief lull following the swish of nylon as hikers have assumed their favored sleeping positions and closed zippered vents, the cacophony starts.

The first offender, situated somewhere on the bunk above me, cycles through a progression of sounds that begins with a throaty snarl, transitions to a series of snorts, and ends with a puffing noise that crescendos with an eerie whistle.

Soon others join the discordance, and for the duration of the night, the rafters reverberate with a din better suited to the wing in hell reserved for apnea sufferers.

I will later meet a thoughtful thru-hiker (and confessed snorer) who proffers ear plugs to all those who slumber near him.

Familiar Ground

ROM RUSSELL FIELD SHELTER, I SET OUT TOWARD ONE OF my favorite destinations in the park: the open meadows of Spence Field and the craggy knob of Rocky Top a mile beyond. I have hiked to this point more than two dozen times over the years, including a particularly memorable winter trek on the heels of an ice storm that had layered the trees in a crystal glaze that shimmered in the sunlight.

This warm, sun-drenched day provides the perfect conditions for ridge-top hiking. I arrive at Spence Field, our first foray above 5,000 feet, to find most of my shelter mates from the previous night lolling in the sun, gobbling snacks, and liberally applying sunscreen. I bypass the Spence Field Shelter, renovated in 2005, and instead join them in the grassy lea before scrambling to the summit of Rocky Top, the inspiration for the popular song allegedly penned in 1967 in nearby Gatlinburg.

To the east looms the 5,527-foot summit of Thunderhead. Below us, to the south, the fingers of Fontana Lake probe into hidden coves. To the northwest, the broad Tennessee Valley rolls out to the horizon.

Engrained Routine

HE NEXT DAY LEADS ME 9.1 MILES TO DERRICK KNOB, making for the toughest going of the entire route, owing to a series of short, thigh-searing ups and downs. Even the thru-hikers, with 200 miles under their boots, complain about the rugged terrain. Here, I meet a southbound thru-hiker, Faithful (David Barnes, 25), from Plymouth, Maine. He is just over two weeks from completion of his quest and bears the look and mien of someone who has spent five months sleeping on the ground—mostly alone through the early months of his journey. He largely keeps to himself and peers off into the woods with a detached though contented gaze.

Tonight, I grab a slot on the top bunk, beneath a skylight, and settle to sleep by the light of an impossibly bright canopy of stars.

The next day, I reach Double Springs Shelter, one of the Smokies' most picturesque camps, set in a spruce forest at 5,507 feet. The following day, I summit Clingmans Dome, my trek's literal high-point.

I emerge from the trail at the base of the Dome's concrete tower and paved walkway, and I'm immediately jarred from my reverie by a charging throng of 100 children dashing for the tower. All are choir and band members from Southside Middle School in St. Petersburg, Florida. They're in Gatlinburg for a competition.

It is my first encounter with folks fresh from the city in nearly a week, and I feel a familiar sense of detachment from them and the world they inhabit.

Over the past week, I've come to savor evenings encamped with new friends and days spent alone, save for the company of warblers and wildflowers and the sweet bite of bee balm and tender ferns hovering on the air.

My camp routine, perfectly engrained during my months on the trail in 1979, has regained its efficiency, and I arrange my bedding and kitchen without a wasted motion. I know by heart the location of nearly all of the items stowed in my pack.

My face bristles with a six-day growth of beard, my sunburned nose and cheeks are beginning to peel, my clothes reek, my fingernails are gritty, but I'm sublimely happy. Though I miss my wife and daughters, the tug of home and its surfeit of nonessential conveniences has eased.

Later in the day, at Mt. Collins Shelter, as my afternoon tea steeps, I lie on my back, watching clouds drift lazily overhead and realize that it has been many months since I afforded myself the luxury of doing *absolutely nothing purposeful*. Thus, I settle into blissful inaction, while thoughts and memories drift through my mind as languidly as the clouds float by overhead. My alter ego, Pangloss, fully approves.

Chef, Soupy, Pete's Draggin', and Day Hiker have pushed on, eager to resupply and binge-eat on city food in Gatlinburg, and I honestly miss their company. Tonight, I share the shelter with Blazing Star (Andi Van Loan, 35), a quiet forestry biologist from Micanopy, Florida.

"I'm out here because I've seen too many people close to me die too early, prompting me to decide that 'now' is 'later'—no more waiting to live my life," she offers as her reason for taking up the trail.

The next morning, I hike the easy 4.5 miles to Newfound Gap, where I'll meet my wife, Belinda, and head into Gatlinburg to re-supply. En route, for the first time in six days, the weather forces me to don my rain jacket and pack cover. The timing of my R&R stop is perfect. While I fortify my body with microbrews and a plate-lopping slab of meat and sleep in a real bed, my colleagues on the trail will contend with one of the fiercest downpours of the season.

We leave Gatlinburg just before dawn the next morning and drive through dense clouds on our way back to Newfound Gap. As we near our destination, we emerge into full sunlight. From the gap, we peer down on a sea of clouds beneath a rising sun.

I've begun to think like a thru-hiker and have shed 10 pounds of extraneous gear—including a digital recorder (never used); a Lexan bowl (never used); the tarp, nylon chord, and four aluminum tent stakes (used once the first night out); flip-flops for wearing around camp (used but not worth the added weight); and a bundle of spare AAA batteries (sufficient voltage to power my headlamp continuously for a month). I've come close to offsetting the added weight of my replenished foodbag. Utra-light champion Day Hiker, for one, would be pleased.

I depart Newfound Gap mindful that my remaining time on the trail is limited and that in two and a half days, I'll meet my wife in Davenport Gap and return to the city, my climate-controlled office, my routine—while my pack will return to its peg in the shed to languish until the next time I break free.

Four miles along the trail, I arrive at the first of the day's spectacular vistas. The rocky knob of Charlies Bunion arches toward blue sky above and vanishes below into the clouds that condemn Gatlinburg to a day of overcast. Beyond, the trail follows a series of narrow ridges, sprinkled with blossoms and tufted with laurel thickets, with views plunging down hundreds of feet into the lingering sea of clouds.

While in Gatlinburg, I learned that my dearest friend lost his mother to cancer during the early days of my trek. I devote the morning to her memory and, as I trod the trail, sing aloud two songs that seem to fit the occasion and setting: "Go Rest High on That Mountain" and "Angel Band." No one is near enough to hear, but I imagine that Mary Ernsting's spirit hovers nearby, appreciative of the gesture and of the copious display of the wildflowers she loved so much.

I reach the spur trail to my home for the night, Pecks Corner Shelter, at 2:00 P.M. Flopped at the junction—deciding whether to stay or push on—is Camel (Tom Horwath, 53), a recovering alcoholic from Ohio and a remarkably spiritual man whose acquaintance I will value as much as any other I make along this journey.

While Camel weighs options, I head down the side trail to the shelter. I have the place to myself—at least for the moment—and immediately set about removing the ragged, olive-drab plastic tarp that someone has draped across the shelter's open face, presumably to keep out the wind. This, one of the beautifully restored AT shelters, deserves a full infusion of afternoon light.

I fill my water bag, inflate my pad, and start my afternoon tea. Almost immediately, I hear the thud of footfalls and look up to see Camel. Later, Pete's Draggin', Chef, Soupy, and Day Hiker bound down the trail to the shelter. Lion King, my campmate during my first night on the trail, arrives near dusk. I'm delighted to see all of them; at least for the evening, my hiking family has reunited. All took two "zero" days (thru-hiker parlance for staying put in town and making no miles) in Gatlinburg, which allowed me to pass them.

By sundown, the shelter will brim to capacity, with five thru-hiker overflow tents erected outside. One cluster of tents houses the five members of the Sierra Club from Dallas, Texas, ranging in age from 51 to 72. Among them is enthusiastic birder Dick Guldi, 64, who will identify a chestnut-sided warbler, confirming my suspicion that the birds that have been faithfully serenading me over my days on the trail are, indeed, the legendary songmeisters, northbounders themselves.

Coming Home

OR MY LAST FULL DAY ON THE TRAIL, LEADING TO COSBY Knob Shelter, I opt to pass the miles in the company of Chef and Soupy. My longest day on the trail—13 miles—is made nearly effortless by virtue of their companionship.

"Ah, you've found your hiking legs," says Chef, noting that I am keeping pace.

We shed our packs for a time at Deer Creek Gap and bask in the sun, savoring the views of Mt. Sterling and Guyot. From here, northbounders won't cross above 6,000 feet again for 150 miles. Beyond the gap, near Inadu Knob, we confront the widely scattered debris of the Air Force F-4 Phantom that crashed here in 1984, killing two crewmen.

Our approach to Cosby Knob is marked by a series of false summits—as we crest each of them, we see a higher peak rising beyond.

"Okay, we've topped Stills, Nash, and Young," quips Chef. "The next one's got to be Cosby."

Soon we arrive at the shelter, my roost for my last night on the trail. Pete's Draggin,' who will meet his girlfriend in Hot Springs, North Carolina, is eager to make miles, and I say goodbye to him.

Chef, Soupy, and I claim our bunk space and set about easing into the afternoon. Day Hiker and Camel arrive a short time later.

As we relax over our cookpots, thru-hiker Grits (Meton Cockrell, 61), an iron-steel worker from Florida, bounds into camp. He is a short, wiry, animated gnome with sun-baked skin the color of raw sienna. Grits is staying just long enough to prepare a meal of ramen noodles and Vienna sausages.

"I'm on my third midlife crises," he tells us. "When you're having a midlife crisis, you get to do stuff like this and people think it's okay." Twenty minutes after arriving, the frenetic Grits has packed up and is back on the trail, heading north for a few more miles before dark.

Later, after dinner, Chef suggests a campfire. Signs posted at all shelters have urged us to "choose not to have a fire," and so far, we have complied. But tonight, we decide to burn some logs.

Despite weary legs, we ignore the arrival of "hiker midnight" and, after dark, gather around a hearty fire. The archetypal effect is almost immediate, and the stories begin to spill from us.

My thoughts have begun to migrate back to the city.

Tomorrow, I will descend 3,025 feet and pass from high mountain ridges still in the grip of winter into Davenport Gap, a forest cloaked in full summer foliage, and beyond, the din of semi-trucks barreling along I-40.

Thoreau responds to my mood by admonishing me to stay put at "the meeting of two eternities." Instead, I abandon the future, bypass the present, and allow my mind to drift back through the decades.

I dwell there for a time, with a young, 23-year-old man who stayed at this shelter nearly 29 years ago, mulling a future that would engender a series of unexpected twists and turns before it would return him to this place as a middle-aged father and husband.

Despite all the changes wrought by the years, these mountains —and the creatures that dwell here—are just as I remember them.

I'm not entirely certain who I will be tomorrow, as I reach the thundering margin of the interstate, or, for that matter, the day after. But this much I do know: Here, tonight, circled by friends' faces glowing in the firelight, I *am* Pangloss.

CHAPTER SEVENTEEN

On the Trail of Benton MacKaye—Again

Three decades ago, two young hikers followed Benton MacKaye's Appalachian Trail from Georgia to Maine. Now, as late-middle-aged dads, they once again follow MacKaye's lead through the Great Smokies along the rugged and remote trail bearing his name.

IT'S MARCH 19, 2012—A TYPICALLY COOL, OCCASIONALLY even snowy, time of year in the Southern Appalachians—but La Niña's lingering influence has progressed from palliative to punishing, with temperatures hovering in the mid-80s. Even the wildflowers seem confused. Spring beauties, blood root, anemones, phlox, trillium, and geranium bloom in profusion along the trail. In a normal year, they'd still be slumbering beneath the leaf litter.

I am at Proctor Field Gap, 3.1 miles from Twentymile Ranger Station in Great Smoky Mountains National Park (GSMNP) on the Benton MacKaye (pronounced *mak-KYE*) Trail (BMT), and the compound adjective "chin-scraping" is about to enter my lexicon of terms useful in describing mountain trails.

The phrase will frequently be of use over the next nine days along the BMT, from Twentymile Ranger Station, where the trail enters the park, to Big Creek, where it ends 94.4 miles later.

The gently ascending grade of a former Jeep road that's led me to this point has suddenly turned sinister. From here, the path tracks uphill at a rate suggesting that the trail's architects, beset by impatience, opted for the most direct of all routes—a straight line—to today's high point on the ridge ahead, Sassafras Gap, at 3,675 feet. We started the day at 1,310 feet.

La Niña's balm seems to have had little influence on the hardwoods, which bear buds but, so far, no shade-producing leaves, and I can feel the tops of my ears beginning to burn. As I struggle, my hiking companion seems to be drawing some crazy energy from the brutal grade and blazing sun.

Dan Howe, assistant city manager for Raleigh, North Carolina, sports a highly visible red T-shirt and becomes an ever-more-remote beacon of fitness as he motors up the mountain. His hours in the saddle of his bicycle—including a 400-mile ride across North Carolina and a jaunt over the Continental Divide at Independence Pass—have clearly paid off.

I'm carrying half our tent, so I know he won't ditch me entirely. As further insurance against abandonment, I'm also toting a flask of aged Puerto Rican rum.

By the time I stumble into Sassafras Gap, Dan has had enough time to drop his pack, temporarily remove his boots, and assemble and half-devour a peanut butter and honey sandwich. Meanwhile, between gasps, I'm mainlining water via the tube from my hydration pack and glancing about for a 20-pound stone that I might surreptitiously slip into Dan's pack to introduce some parity to our venture.

The Same but Different

THIS ISN'T THE FIRST TIME DAN AND I HAVE EMBARKED ON a journey on foot along a route that bears the imprimatur—and, in this case, the name—of one of our heroes.

Back in 1921, Benton MacKaye, the Harvard-educated forester, conservationist, and visionary, conceived of a trail extending along the Appalachian spine. By 1937, the Appalachian Trail route was complete.

In 1979 Dan and I walked MacKaye's trail, all 2,100-plus miles of it, seeking to escape an America that had confronted the momentous challenges of the 1960s and early 1970s only to return to an eerie and disappointing stasis.

When I took up the trail, I was long on ambition, but woefully lacking in experience; I had backpacked only once or twice. Dan's route to the AT was a bit different. A former jet-setting planner for a major oil company, Dan had swapped his fancy suits for a Camp Trails external-frame backpack and a pair of stout Fabiano boots.

Dan, who had attended college in Virginia, in the shadow of the Appalachians, made frequent forays into the mountains, and he took up the AT physically and mentally tough and possessed of a set of backwoods skills that only emphasized my lack.

I spent the first difficult days on the trail struggling to keep pace and experiencing emotions that ranged from awe to loathing toward Dan's exquisite competence. Eventually, my proficiency grew, and I began to regard Dan as a guy who's quick to laugh, rock steady in a crisis, as generous with his thoughts as he was with the items he carried in his pack, and ravenous to learn as much as he could about the wilds that spread around us. As I recall, he toted one weighty book devoted to Eastern wildflowers and another on birds.

For 21 weeks, Dan and I marched north from Springer Mountain, Georgia, to Mt. Katahdin, Maine. We were 23 and lean (and, by trail's end, long-haired and bearded). Much of what we valued we carried on our backs, and we bore little responsibility beyond reaching Maine before we had burned through our cash reserves.

That was then.

Dan and I are now late-middle-aged dads with graying beards and bearing mountains of responsibility, compared with our care-free days on the AT, along with thousands of dollars worth of high-end backpacking gear that would have stunned and amazed us in 1979. Back then, boots weighed five pounds, state of the art in raingear was a flapping poncho, and wool was still the insulating fabric of choice.

Dan has agreed to accompany me on what will be our first extended backpacking trip in 33 years.

For me, it's a working gig, and I experience an occasional pang of guilt for having persuaded Dan to join me on a hike that, over the first few days, will involve far more rigor than reward.

Prior to our departure, I received an understated email from Bob Ruby, one of the BMT Association's board members, alerting me to "quite a bit of vertical" along the trail route. In fact, according to Ruby, the BMT involves 55 percent more vertical gain and loss than the AT section through the park, which, in 1979, proved challenging enough, even for two 23-year-olds with 163 trail miles under their boots.

Our itinerary, shaped primarily by Dan's allotment of annual leave, will subject us to several 12-plus mile days, some of which will be daylight-consuming endeavors.

Dan, having finished his peanut butter sandwich, is back in his boots and on his feet, indicating his interest in moving on. After a break that, in my estimation, is all too short, an abrupt 3.2-mile plunge from Sassafras Gap leads us to Campsite 90, where Lost Cove Creek—our water source—spills into a long finger of Fontana Lake.

The campsite has seen its share of use, and a smattering of non-combustibles left by former residents litter the iron fire ring, but our chosen tent site is tabletop flat, and the rhododendrons that crowd the clearing provide sparse but welcome shade.

As I filter water, Dan erects our domicile, an ample three-person dome tent. Big is good, particularly when it comes to tents. Dan and I have both spent more than our share of nights confined to cramped, fetid nylon structures allegedly large enough to accommodate two, provided the pair are either undernourished adolescents or "intimate"—neither description applies to us. Our camp digs will be spacious, but good sleep will elude me for most of the trek, owing to a last-minute and poorly advised compromise to save weight.

Later, as I roll out my $10, wafer-thin discount-store foam sleeping pad, I watch Dan inflate an air mattress so lush and thick he could sleep atop an engine block without registering the slightest discomfort.

The Fireman

AN, A PLANNER BY TRAINING, BRINGS A HIGH LEVEL OF precision to all of his pursuits, but his fire-building methodology borders on an obsession. Tonight, like most nights, Dan assembles orderly stacks of dried wood, progressing from kindling to thigh-thick chunks, before configuring twigs into a perfectly symmetrical teepee.

I can tell that the mysterious four-foot section of railroad track jutting from the fire ring is seriously messing with his *feng shui*, but he manages to work around the obstacle and sets the structure ablaze with a single match.

Over our months on the AT, Dan and I dodged the smoke and poked the coals of hundreds of campfires. This one, like all the others, inspires contented reflection. Tonight's topic is the AT's best sections (a list on which we're in total agreement): Maine's isolated, roadless 100-mile Wilderness, which courses past pristine backcountry lakes from Monson to Abol Bridge, near the base of the trail's final mountain (for northbounders), Katahdin. The rugged White Mountains and particularly Mount Washington, from whose summit we were able to glimpse the Atlantic shore 75 miles away. And, of course, GSMNP, with its abundance of flowing water and ecozones so lush and green they almost looked fake.

As we cycle through the AT's "best-of" list, I find my memories still vivid and alive. With no effort, I close my eyes, tumble back through 33 years, and can "see" us, clad in our now-antique gear and moving through each of the coveted sections of trail.

In all the scenes, Dan is skinny (I am, too), wearing that buffalo-plaid wool shirt, the smoke- and dirt-smudged canvas hat pulled low above his eyes, and the gnarled walking stick clutched in his right hand.

On the first day of our hike, Dan had scoured the top of Spring Mountain searching for a walking stick that would accompany him all the way to Maine. His ultimate selection was functional but in no way beautiful, and I still can't account for how or why he chose it. Nevertheless, Dan's relationship with the stick was as enduring as it was monogamous, and he suffered greatly in New Hampshire to ensure that it remained in his possession.

On the trail, just north of Hanover, Dan walked right over a two-foot hole in the ground seething with angry yellow jackets. The assault lasted less than a minute, but it resulted in more than 20 stings. In the aftermath, Dan sat quietly on a rock a safe distance from the swarming bees, gathered himself, and then began *walking back toward the nest*. Thinking that the venom had, by now, entered his brain and impaired his judgment, I moved to stop him.

"I dropped my walking stick," is all he said, as he pushed past me. The stick lay a foot from the nest, and he was forced to crawl on his belly the last few yards to retrieve it. With the stick back in his grasp, he slipped into his pack, turned to me, and said, "Let's go."

At the end of our trek, on the top of Mt. Katahdin, Dan disappeared for a few minutes and returned without his stick. "I had a little private ceremony," he explained. As far as I known, the stick that had traveled all the way from Georgia is still up there somewhere, nestled among the rocks.

For our current trek, while I lean on high-end trekking poles, Dan employs yet another gnarly wooden staff. He acquired this one—a section of maple contorted into a corkscrew shape by a honeysuckle vine—from a friend whose grandfather had died and left the stick leaning against the wall on his front porch.

The fire is burning low, and Dan stirs the coals before we head to bed. In the morning, we will connect with and follow the Lakeshore Trail and pass though a section of the park steeped in history—and conflict. Had things turned out differently, we might have been treading on blacktop, rather than dirt and rock, as we trace the north shore of Fontana Lake.

In the early 1940s, the Tennessee Valley Authority acquired about 60,000 acres of land to build Fontana Dam and power the aluminum smelters producing materials for World War II. Hundreds of families were displaced by the project.

Small communities with names like Proctor and Bone Valley were cut off by or disappeared entirely below the rising waters when the dam was completed in 1944. Also submerged was N.C. Highway 288, which connected Bryson City to Deals Gap and served as the main route of travel along the northern shore of the Little Tennessee and Tuckasegee Rivers in Swain County, North Carolina.

Swain County had incurred considerable debt in constructing the road and sought compensation from the federal government. In a 1943 agreement among TVA, Swain County, the state of North Carolina, and the U.S. Department of the Interior (DOI), TVA turned over 44,400 acres to DOI, and the land became part of GSMNP and now includes more than 40 miles of the Benton MacKaye Trail.

DOI, in turn, agreed to build a new road through the park, along the north shore of Fontana Lake. By the early 1960s, about six miles of the road had been completed. Construction progressed no further, because of fiscal as well as economic, engineering, and environmental issues.

For decades, The Road to Nowhere, as it became known, sustained a bitter dispute between opponents, who, on the one hand, wanted to preserve one of the largest remaining tracts of unbroken wilderness in the Southeast, and, on the other, those favoring construction of the road, as promised, including residents of Swain County.

Finally, in February 2010, Interior Secretary Ken Salazar announced a settlement whereby DOI would pay up to $52 million into a trust fund established for Swain County, in lieu of building the road.

Water World

 LONG ITS FIRST 63 MILES THROUGH THE PARK, TO SMOKE-mont Campground, the BMT explores a world defined by water.

From Campsite 90, we soon reach the edge of surging Eagle Creek and, out of habit, peer up and down stream for a footbridge, before it dawns on us that the remote BMT might not feature such luxuries.

I'm wearing high-top Gore-Tex-lined boots and manage a convulsive hop across the creek on slick, moss-covered rocks. Dan, whose boots are not waterproof, is forced to don his camp shoes—a pair of knock-off Tevas that look better suited to a Sarasota shuffleboard match than a stream ford—before sloshing across to join me on the other side.

Over the next several days, we will frequently repeat the process—often with both of us forced to peel off our boots—before wading across knee-deep streams, some bearing names on the map, others not, but all brimming with cold spring runoff.

Near the junction with the Lakeshore Trail, we encounter a group of fellow hikers, college students from Knoxville, who have erected their tents amid a cluster of huge boulders on a grassy floodplain. Their campsite will soon lie under water when TVA stoppers the spillway and restores Fontana Lake—now rimmed by a meandering 20-foot band of parched ocher dirt—to its summer water levels.

A few miles beyond, a rusted steel bridge leads us across Hazel Creek to the remains of Proctor, a once-thriving community that became a casualty to Fontana Lake's rising waters in 1944. Established in 1886 as a farming community, Proctor became a boomtown in 1910 when the W. M. Ritter Lumber Company built a mill here. In its heyday, Proctor boasted a population of 1,000 served by a dentist, a doctor, and a barber, and its main street featured a café, a school house, and a movie theater.

Proctor's fortunes began to fade when Ritter departed in 1928. Sixteen years later, Fontana Lake swallowed up much of the surviving community. What was left, including the community's cemetery, became stranded when the lake's rising waters spilled across N.C. Highway 288, which had served as the main route of travel for the families and merchants occupying the northern shore of the Little Tennessee and Tuckasegee Rivers.

The remnants of Proctor include a fragmented and rusting Model A Ford and the largely intact Calhoun house, a tidy white-washed clapboard structure whose ample porch and open front door seem to suggest that its former residents might return home at any minute.

Along the lake shore, we share the path with few other hikers, but we're hardly alone; evidence of alien invaders abounds around nearly ever bend in the trail. Skeletal remains of hemlocks, most covered with blue-green lichen, reveal the work of the hemlock woolly adelgid. *Adelges tsugae Annand,* an aphid-like insect native to Asia, was first confirmed in GSMNP in May 2002 and has since seen wide distribution throughout the park. We notice a few hemlocks that seem to be thriving in defiance of the invasive pests. We learn later, from a forester, that the park staff has launched an aggressive effort to treat and save many of the specimen trees, particularly in backcountry campsites, with imported predator beetles and pesticides. The latter, though effective, must be applied every two years.

Sus scofa has been here, too. The wild hog native to Europe escaped its confines on Hooper Bald, North Carolina, more than 60 years ago and has since colonized the park. The hogs' foraging for plant roots and bulbs has left wide swaths of excavated soil along the trail.

We also see evidence of an equally pesky but native insect, the southern pine beetle. In the late 1990s, the beetle encountered vast stands of yellow pine, particularly in the western section of the park, and went into a feeding and breeding frenzy, leaving in its wake tangles of toppled trees.

The End of the Road

OR TWO DAYS, WE HUG THE LAKE SHORE, AND THE RELA-tively gentle terrain allows us to adjust to load-bearing without the added burden of long climbs. En route to Campsite 74, at the mouth of Forney Creek, we puzzle over an odd but orderly heap of well-used water shoes at the lip of a foot bridge, hike past an empty wild hog trap, and confront an inelegant but functional backwoods privy, featuring a toilet seat balanced precariously atop a five-gallon bucket.

Just beyond, we reach the campsite and, after erecting the tent and filtering water, splash in the frigid creek and hang our sweat-soaked clothes out to dry. We note, with some regret, that the rum supply is running low.

Later that evening, a consuming mania to trim pack weight and keep pace with Dan drives me to commit contemptible acts—not least of which is book burning. Henry Beston's *Outermost House* and a spare notebook kindle the flames of Dan's evening campfire.

For the next couple of hours, we bask in the firelight, sipping the last of the rum from a plastic bottle and following our memories back more than three decades, to a time of sublime freedom and happiness, when all we really needed was contained in our 35-pound packs and when two-by-six-inch white paint blazes directed our path north, toward Maine.

We recall, in particular, the friends we made that summer.

Nick, the Michigan Granddad, at 57, was 10 years older than my father. Paul, the agile, long-legged former competitive skier, joined us somewhere in New Jersey. Cathy, one of the few female thru-hikers we encountered over the summer, traveled with a burly and aggressive German shepherd who ultimately convinced us to abandon any hopes of pursuing a romantic relationship. Elizabeth, a middle-aged widow, had taken up the trail to grieve the loss of her husband.

The cascade of memories has an unexpected influence on me, and, I sense, on Dan, too. We cherish our wives and children—and speak of them often—and are grateful for careers that have afforded us secure and comfortable lives. But our reflections haunt as much as they entertain, reminding us of lost youth and the reality that we will never again experience a life so simple, carefree, and uncluttered.

Though our AT experiences continue to shape and define us, even after all these years, we both learned long ago that the AT's nomadic lifestyle is not particularly portable nor are the skills it hones directly applicable in the world beyond the margins of the foot path. At trail's end all those years ago, Dan and I returned— with some resentment and even a bit of awkwardness—to the society we had left behind. For me, initial efforts to resurrect the tenor and meaning of that wonderful summer through weekend backpacking trips proved disappointing, until I learned to recognize that the trail had exposed me to a whole new way of living and seeing—a great gift so few have the opportunity to experience. Nevertheless, as Dan stirs the coals, I find myself wondering what might result if, when we reach the end of the BMT in a few days, we just kept walking.

I zip into my sleeping bag, feeling a twinge of sadness, hopeful that the transformative power of nature will, once again, work its magic on both of us, leaving us grateful for, and not wistful over, the lives we once led.

The next morning, at the junction with the Goldmine Loop Trail, we encounter a flyer, sealed in a clear plastic bag and pinned to the trail sign, announcing the disappearance of Derek Lueking, 24, of Blount County, Tennessee. The flyer confirms the rumors that have been passing among backcountry travelers over the past few days. On March 17, two days before Dan and I began our trek,

Leuking abandoned his SUV in the Newfound Gap parking lot—and, with it, what little camping gear he had brought with him. A note left in the vehicle indicated that Leuking did not want to be found.

Lueking's desire not to be found did not, of course, relieve the National Park Service staff of its obligation to hunt for him. We will learn later that an intensive week-long search, which will involve hundreds of park staff and volunteers, a team of Tennessee Department of Correction officers with tracking dogs, and two helicopters, will fail to locate the missing Lueking, who, some suspect, wandered into the woods on a suicidal mission.

It wouldn't be the first time a distraught individual had entered GSMNP on a one-way trip. In fact, in January 2012, rangers investigated two apparent suicides in the park. In the first instance, the victim apparently logged his own 911 call, alerting officials of a suicide note attached to the dashboard of a vehicle parked in the Newfound Gap parking lot and of a lifeless body on the ground just below the overlook. From there, the 56-year-old Florida man apparently ended the call and fulfilled his own prophecy.

Ten days later, park officials responded to a report from hikers who found a body lying in a pool of blood on the Bradley Fork Trail, a third of a mile from the Smokemont Campground. A .40 caliber handgun positioned near the body indicated the apparent cause of death.

If the flyer featuring Lueking's photo is unsettling, what we encounter next borders on the surreal. The fact that the North Shore Road was never completed does not mean it wasn't started. Three miles from camp we abruptly step onto an incongruous stretch of blacktop—the official end to the Road to Nowhere. Just beyond, we enter an equally strange 1,200-foot-long tunnel, its drab masonry face and interior walls scrawled with colorful graffiti.

We emerge into daylight and soon reach a trailhead parking lot and meet four male members of the White family, ranging in age from 27 to 65, who have just finished a loop hike. We graciously accept their offer of cold beers. I roll the cans in my foam sleeping pad and stopper the ends with spare socks to keep them chilled for later.

We arrive at the Bald Creek Campsite under darkening skies and a break from the searing sun. The 7.5-mile, 1,700-foot climb that led us here was challenging but not daunting. Our muscles seem to have recovered their now three-decade-old memory, and our consumption of food has lightened our loads. I regard the added weight of the icy beers from the White family as a boon, not a burden.

Blessed Be the Calvinists

AIN PEPPERS OUR TENT THROUGH THE NIGHT, REVEALING a troubling chink in the dome's ripstop nylon armor. We're both carrying down sleeping bags—yet another weight-saving measure—and rain will be a prominent feature over our next few days and nights on the trail.

The next morning, we dodge raindrops through a hasty breakfast, pack a wet tent, and set out in a light drizzle. Dan's eager to field test his new rainwear; I opt to hike wet and dry out later. The mild temperature poses little threat of hypothermia, and my rain jacket and fleece are within easy reach in my pack, should I need them.

A mile beyond camp, at the junction with the Nolan Divide Trail, we meet nine spring breakers from Calvin College in Grand Rapids, Michigan. They're hard to miss: They've set up their two outsized dome tents in the middle of the trail. Our encounter with them will later prove fortuitous.

On assignment for *Smokies Life* magazine in 2009, I hiked the Mountains to Sea Trail, including an eight-mile section of the BMT, where the two share the same route, and I now see no need to retrace my steps, particularly after the persistent drizzle has morphed into a torrential downpour.

Dan and I shamelessly succumb to the lure of civilization and decide to depart the BMT and hike out to Deep Creek picnic area. From there, we'll take our chances on finding a ride into Cherokee.

Over the last few miles, the trail itself becomes a churning creek, and though my pack is secure under a waterproof cover, my shirt and shorts are plastered to my body. With each step, water gurgles out through the leather of my sodden boots.

Once at the picnic area, we cower under the narrow eave of a bathhouse, its door still locked for the season, as the young Calvinists arrive sequentially behind us and gather around their van. We slosh slowly over to greet them, and our effort to project an abject level of misery, suffering, and need—carefully honed over our months on the AT—has the desired effect. The spring breakers offer us a lift into town.

Dan and I check into the Microtel in Cherokee and at the front desk notice a stack of flyers bearing Derek Lueking's smiling face. Security cameras showed Lueking leaving the hotel at 4 A.M. on March 17—the last known sighting—and his family members have amassed here to continue the search.

After hot showers, we binge eat at a Mexican restaurant, watch some NCAA basketball, and sleep on soft beds. The next morning, a hotel maid shuttles us to Smokemont Campground, where we resume our hike, initially by walking a mile *in the wrong direction* along a footway churned to muck by horses. In the interest of full disclosure, our detour into Cherokee will deprive me of 4.7 miles of the BMT (from Newton Bald to Smokemont), so I can't rightfully claim to have thru-hiked the trail through the park.

Once Dan discovers his error, he channels his frustration through his thighs and vanishes up the trail. I'll find him nearly seven miles and 2,700 vertical feet later, at the junction with the Enloe Creek Trail. As I approach Dan, I am delighted to see that serenity has returned to his face, as a peanut butter sandwich disappears into his eager maw. "Sorry," he says, between bites. "I just had to get that out of my system."

From here, we'll remain above 3,000 feet, passing through mist-shrouded fir and spruce forests, crossing the headwaters of remote creeks, and reaching our high point of 5,842 feet atop Mt. Sterling.

The Enloe Creek Campsite is barely large enough to accommodate two tents, and since one camper has already claimed his spot, we settle for an angled, rock-studded clearing barely large enough for our tent's ample hips. The campsite's dominant feature, a waterfall thundering over huge boulders into a deep plunge pool, is the main attraction for the other tent's owner, Cliff Williams, an attorney from Cartersville, Georgia.

Williams soon saunters into camp wearing chest waders and clutching a fly rod. He reports that the fishing is good and that he managed to catch a brook trout and a rainbow on a single leader bearing two flies. He shows us a photo on his point-and-shoot camera to prove it.

Williams is one of several fishermen we've encountered on the BMT, which explores some of the more secluded (read, hard to get to) and productive trout fisheries in the park. Though dusk is but an hour away, Williams announces that he's hiking out and will cover more than three miles, with his heavy load, back to his car. He breaks down his tent and fly rod and is gone in 10 minutes.

Once again, we have the campsite to ourselves, but the rain has us ducking for cover. Dan and I seek shelter and cook and eat dinner under the sturdy bridge spanning the creek. Later, when we're in our sleeping bags, the dome tent, once again, begins to drool on us, and we're forced to cover our down sleeping bags with our rain jackets. I will awaken to find my feet swaddled in wad of wet feathers.

The BMT may be water-rich, but it's bereft of open mountain-top vistas for nearly its entire length through the park. Tomorrow, we realize, that will begin to change, after we ascend nearly 2,500 feet to Laurel Gap Shelter and the gateway to the Mt. Sterling Ridge, where the trail remains above 5,000 feet.

Laurel Gap Shelter, nestled in a grassy clearing below mature spruce and hardwoods, bears no resemblance to the dank, dingy GSMNP shelters we recall from our days on the AT. The shelter is open and airy, and a skylight brightens the interior space through the day and, by night, provides hikers a view of the heavens. Most notably, gone is the chain-link barrier that once separated hikers from marauding bears in this and other park shelters.

The shelter's renovation, funded by a coalition of partners, including Friends of the Smokies, was completed in December 2011 and marks the end of a multi-year effort to renovate all 15 back-country shelters in the park.

For the first time along our trek, we will share our home for the night with other hikers. Emily Francis, 30, is an events manager with Full Steam Brewery in Durham, North Carolina. She and Sarah Wylie, 28, a public health professional, also from Durham, are out on an ambitious but largely unstructured two-week trek. The only fixed appointment on their schedule is a planned rendez-vous with their husbands in a few days in Hot Springs, North Carolina. Paul White, 55, a software developer from Atlantic Beach, North Carolina, is on a multi-day solo hike.

During Dan's and my months on the AT, shelters served as so-cial hubs, and we almost always welcomed the company—along with the wide-ranging discussions that easily transitioned from food fantasies to favored articles of gear to home towns. Here, at Laurel Gap Shelter, the conversation follows a similar tack.

Dan, Emily, and Sarah swap details about restaurants in the Research Triangle. Paul discusses the joys and challenges of work-ing from an in-home office near the shore. Emily's detailed de-scriptions of Full Steam's crafted beers only accentuate our glaring lack.

My envy of Dan's air mattress only deepens when I learn that Emily has one, too.

Stiff winds and temperatures in the 40s force Dan and me to don every article of clothing in our packs. The fleece jackets, ther-mal base layers, wool caps, and gloves have languished in our packs for the past seven days, and we're delighted finally to be able to justify their added weight.

At dawn, sun pours into the shelter's open face, and Dan and I begin to rouse. "You snored all night," I tell him. "You did, too!" he replies. I'm certain he's wrong but see no need to press the point.

Emily and Sarah are still with us, but Paul departed at daybreak. From here, we face an easy six-mile lope along the ridge that we know will deliver us to Mt. Sterling, its ancient firetower, and, for the first time, views of the surrounding mountains.

Our early arrival on Mt. Sterling entitles us to first dibs on highly coveted Campsite 38, situated at the base of the firetower. Soon, it becomes clear that our relatively solitary march is over, as the first of dozens of hikers arrive in the clearing, including the U.S. Army Field Band, out for a couple of days of R&R.

Our division of labor assigns Dan tent-erecting duties, while water-gathering is left to me and my seriously clogged filter, which has turned the nightly task into a painful isometric exercise. If water is abundant along most of the BMT, it's notably scarce up here. A sign directs me toward a spring that's nearly half a mile downhill.

En route, clutching empty water bag, bottles, and a cook pot, I succumb to the beauty that sprawls around me and slow my pace. Tomorrow, it's down the mountain and back to the world. Once there, I know I'll wish I had spent more time taking in all that's here.

The rain is gone, but it has inspired an explosion of lush green. The wildflowers, more than adequately watered and now drinking in the sunshine, teem in greater abundance than I've ever seen. White trilliums blanket entire hillsides, violets cluster beside downed trees, and spring beauties form an endless snowy carpet.

In half an hour, I've filled all the empty vessels from the piped spring and stand to begin the trek back to camp, but a desire to linger inclines me to settle back on the ground and bask for a time in the beauty that surrounds me. Gone are any concerns about crippling mishaps, missed trail junctions, or any of the myriad other things that might have kept us from finishing our hike.

It's the finishing that begins to gnaw at me. At the outset of our hike, nine days seemed such a generous allotment of time, particularly for two family men with demanding careers and calendar pages choked with scheduled appointments. But we're also former long-distance hikers once conditioned to think in terms of months, not days, of adventure and covering a trail whose distance is measured in thousands, not hundreds, of miles.

In April of 1979, Dan and I stood on Springer Mountain, Georgia, and peered north along a path that, we knew, would provide ample time and space to evolve, change, and discover the most fundamental truths about ourselves, each other, and the natural world that sprawled around us.

As I rise to return to camp, I realize that the evolving, changing, and discovering are ongoing processes and that our nine days on the BMT will, even if in barely perceptible ways, nudge us forward and perhaps lend new perspective on all that awaits us back home. Benton MacKaye would have expected nothing less. In his 1921 paper that proposed creation of a trail along the crest of the Appalachian Mountains, he articulated the dividends of wilderness experience this way:

> Life for two weeks on the mountain top would show up many things about life during the other fifty weeks down below. The latter could be viewed as a whole—away from its heat, and sweat, and irritations. There would be a chance to catch a breath, to study the dynamic forces of nature and the possibilities of shifting to them the burdens now carried on the backs of men.

Back in camp, the interlopers begin to intrude on *our* space and climb *our* firetower, though after eight days of relative isolation, we're happy to have the company. The least congruous visitor is Shane Thread, a physics and chemistry teacher from a charter school in Evansville, Indiana, who dashes into the clearing wearing a sweat-drenched gray T-shirt, running shorts, and a vest that we can only surmise carries tubes of energy elixir—and not hand grenades—in its bulging pockets.

Thread, under the influence of surging endorphins, fills us in. He's run up from Big Creek, covering the six miles and 4,000 vertical feet in one hour and 14 minutes. As the sun begins to track toward the horizon, we express concern about sufficient daylight to see him back down. "No problem. Should be down in 42 minutes," he says. Then he's gone.

Later, a half hour before sundown, Dan and I climb to the wind-buffeted top of the firetower and watch a long, jagged shadow swallow up the mountains to the east. Shortly after, the sun nestles into the notched massif of 6,621-foot Mt. Guyot, and a sash of crimson spreads across the western horizon. Later still, the dense clusters of lights marking the houses and roads of Waynesville and Ashville began to wink to the east.

All trails end, even the 2,100-milers, and reaching the terminus is always bittersweet. Sweet to return home to loved ones, to scrub days of accumulated grit from your body, to sup on foods that don't need to be reconstituted with two cups of boiling water, and to sleep on clean sheets and soft mattresses.

The bitter is a bit more complicated. Friendships, particularly those that have been forged over many months and thousands of miles of trail, are precious and profoundly durable.

Backpackers are well advised to exercise prudence in choosing their companions. The rigors of life on the trail can chafe, particularly when the inevitable snags intrude on even the most perfectly planned outing, and the water filter clogs, tent seams leak, a hasty glance at a map sends you a mile or two along a rugged trail in exactly the wrong direction, or buckets of rain infuse your boots with water cold enough to chill a can of beer.

Over the course of our nine days along the Benton MacKaye Trail through GSMN, Dan and I contended with all those. Yet, neither of us would have characterized them as hardship.

Hardship is idling in rush hour traffic, sitting in a climate-controlled office and peering through glass at the awakening spring, or running your finger along the thin line of a trail on a topo map and *not* having the freedom to explore it with your feet.

I recalled a particular pause, a few days earlier, amid a pounding downpour at the edge of a swollen river, one of many that would require us to shed our boots. Conditions were such that I couldn't imagine a less pleasant day to be traveling on foot through the mountains.

Then I caught a glimpse of Dan's smiling face peering out from beneath his rain-pummeled parka hood.

Though he didn't say a word, I knew exactly what he was thinking. I was thinking it, too: "A bit of rough going, sure, but there's no place I'd rather be."

Reading List

Appalachian Odyssey, Steve Sherman and Julia Older. South Greene Press.

The Appalachian Trail Reader, David Emblidge (ed.). Oxford University Press, USA.

Blind Courage, Bill Irwin. McCasland.

The Complete Walker, Colin Fletcher. Alfred A. Knopf, Inc.

Desert Solitaire, Edward Abbey. Touchstone.

Desire and Ice, David Brill. National Geographic Adventure Press.

The Forest Unseen, David George Haskell. Penguin Books.

Leaves of Grass, Walt Whitman. Modern Library

Hiking the Appalachian Trail, James R. Hare. Rodale Press.

The Maine Woods, Henry David Thoreau. Penguin Books.

The Man Who Walked through Time, Colin Fletcher. Random House.

The Monkey-Wrench Gang, Edward Abbey. Avon Books.

The Nick Adams Stories, Ernest Hemingway. Charles Scribner's Sons.

On the Beaten Path, Robert Alden Rubin. The Lyons Press.

On the Road, Jack Kerouac. Penguin Publishing.

The Oregon Trail, Francis Parkman. Oxford University Press.

Pilgrim at Tinker Creek, Annie Dillard. Harper and Row.

The Road, Cormac McCarthy. Vintage Books.

Sand Country Almanac, Aldo Leopold. Ballantine Books.

A Separate Place, David Brill. Plume.

A Short Walk in the Hindu Kush, Eric Newby. Lonely Planet.

The Snow Leopard, Peter Matthiessen. Penguin Publishing.

The Spirit of the Appalachian Trail: Community, Environment, and Belief, Susan Bratton. University of Tennessee Press.

A Thousand-Mile Walk to the Gulf, John Muir. Mariner Books.

Walden, Henry David Thoreau. Doubleday & Company, Inc.

Walk across America, Peter Jenkins. Fawcett Juniper.

Walk West, Peter and Barbara Jenkins. William Morrow and Company.

Walking with Spring, Earl Shaffer. Appalachian Trail Conference.

A Woman's Journey, Cindy Ross. Appalachian Trail Conference.

Zen and the Art of Motorcycle Maintenance, Robert M. Pirsig. Bantam Books.